TOPICAL
STAMP COLLECTING

TOPICAL
STAMP COLLECTING

M. W. MARTIN

ARCO PUBLISHING COMPANY, INC.
219 Park Avenue South, New York, N.Y. 10003

Published by Arco Publishing Company, Inc.
219 Park Avenue South, New York, New York 10003

Library of Congress Catalog Card Number 74-19793
ISBN 0-668-03754-7 (Library Edition)
ISBN 0-668-03662-1 (Paper Edition)

Printed in the United States of America

Contents

Foreword		ix
Introduction		xi
1.	Advertising	3
2.	Agriculture	7
3.	Airlines and Civil Aviation	9
4.	Americana	13
5.	Animals	15
6.	Art	19
7.	Automobiles	21
8.	Banks and Banking	25
9.	Basketball	27
10.	Bicycles and Cycling	31
11.	Birds	33
12.	Chess	37
13.	Christmas	39
14.	Computers and EDP	43
15.	Construction Industry	45
16.	Dentistry	49
17.	Electric Power Industry	51
18.	Flowers	55
19.	Gems and Minerals	57
20.	Golf	61
21.	Graphic Arts Industry	62
22.	Guns	65
23.	Horses and Horse Racing	69
24.	Ice Skating	71
25.	Insects	75
26.	Iron and Steel Industries	77
27.	Judaica	81

28.	Law and the Legal Profession	83
29.	Lions International	87
30.	Masonry	89
31.	Medicine	93
32.	Mining	95
33.	Money	99
34.	Music	101
35.	New York City	105
36.	Nursing	107
37.	Petroleum Industry	111
38.	Pharmacy and the Pharmaceutical Industry	113
39.	Police	117
40.	Railroads	121
41.	Scouting	123
42.	Ships	127
43.	Space Exploration	129
44.	Sports	133
45.	Telephone and Telecommunications	137
46.	Textile Industry	139
47.	Trucks and the Trucking Industry	143
48.	Veterinary Medicine	145
49.	Weight Lifting	149
50.	Yachting and Boating	151
51.	How to Form a Topical Stamp Collection	154
52.	Where to Get Stamps, Stamp Catalogs, Albums and Supplies	156
53.	Where to Get Handbooks, Checklists, and Other Topical Information	158

Foreword

The author of this book invited me to write this foreword to his work, and I do so with the greatest pleasure. Much has been written extolling the delights of topical stamp collecting, but Mr. Martin's book is different from all that have gone before. In the past Mr. Martin has written hundreds of articles and columns describing the many "faces" of postage stamps. Drawing on this extensive experience, he has put together a splendid presentation of the 50 most popular stamp topics in the world. Each chapter of this book covers a different subject portrayed on stamps; each chapter is accompanied by a page of photos of representative stamps; and each chapter gives the reader a clear, brief, and interesting introduction to that particular topic. At the end of the book, three excellent chapters clearly and fully inform the reader how to start his own topical collection.

Topical stamp collecting is *the* hobby of the day. No other hobby allows the collector to develop his individuality to such an extent or through such a wide range. Topicals are economical, procurable, and one's collection original-assembled is the only one of its kind! Collecting topicals offers barrels of fun on a small budget, fits in perfectly with vocation or hobbies, affords opportunity for research, encourages delightful correspondence with collectors in distant places, and adds joy and zest to living.

Those who read Mr. Martin's book will quickly learn how to enjoy the world's fastest growing hobby: topical stamp collecting.

Jerome Husak
Founder, American
Topical Association

Introduction

Topical collecting is collecting stamps according to the subject portrayed on the stamps. It's easy to become a topical stamp collector. Just pick a topic of interest and collect only stamps that are related to that specific subject.

Topical stamp collecting has been growing at a phenomenal rate in the last few years. Men and women from every walk of life are attracted to topicals in a manner unequalled by any hobby.

To almost everyone, topical collecting has one outstanding appeal: it is FUN. Topical collecting is fun for the collector because it frees him from the torture of getting every stamp that is issued, regardless of price, or failing that, from explaining the many empty places in the album. It is also fun for the non-collector who views your album: It makes sense, it tells a story, it's not a hodge-podge of empty spaces separated by a few stamps; it's COMPLETE at all times. True, you may miss many stamps pertaining to your topic, but your friends will never know that a species or two are lacking in your flower bouquet, if, for example, you have decided to collect Flowers on Stamps.

Topical collecting has another outstanding appeal: the ability to select a subject that is of strong interest to the selector. A former athlete might have little interest in stamps as such, but when exposed to stamps picturing sports, may very well become an ardent collector. The stamps may bring back old memories, or serve to interest others in the sports they picture. The nature enthusiast, the traveller, and the devotee of fine arts will all find topical subjects to supplement their main hobby. Historians, doctors, lawyers, clergymen, teachers, writers, engineers—these and others often become interested in stamps relating to their professions or work.

It is readily seen that the selection of a topic is limited only by the imagination. Topical collecting has no set rules, no lengthy lists of "dos and don'ts." Undoubtedly this appeals to many people who never gave stamp collecting so much as a thought until they were exposed to topicals.

The educational value of stamps has been recognized since the first stamp collection was formed. Unfortunately the average stamp collection appeals to only a few people, mostly other stamp collectors, but a topical collection has popular appeal through the beauty of the stamps and the related story they tell. History, art, religion, transportation, biology, music, sciences—everything is depicted on today's stamps. Teachers, editors, clergymen, radio, and TV program directors all have been quick to recognize the educational value of stamps and particularly topical collections of stamps. Business firms have used topical stamps in advertising, and a few have used displays of these stamps to call attention to their manufactured products in trade shows and fairs.

The actual mechanics of getting started on the collection are very simple. Go through the 50 topics listed in this book, decide what you like best, and turn to Chapter 51 for complete instructions on how to form a topical stamp collection.

M. W. Martin

TOPICAL
STAMP COLLECTING

1. Advertising

Though private advertising on postage stamps is unknown in some parts of the world—notably in the United States—the practice is almost as old as stamps themselves and is widely used around the globe.

The first to use stamps for advertising was the British Pears' Soap Company which marketed a "transparent soap" invented by Andrew Pears. In 1887, they started to print the words "Use Pears Soap" on the backs of unused postage stamps. This was done without permission and against the rules of the Post Office, but even after the firm was warned to cease and desist they continued to buy the stamps, print them, and give them as souvenirs.

New Zealand was the first government to seriously consider selling the space on the backs of their stamps to commercial advertisers. Official offers for bids for space appeared in 1891, and various advertisers purchased space for ads which shortly appeared announcing a large variety of products. Interesting collections can be formed of these advertisements at moderate cost. Particularly popular with collectors of these advertisements is the reconstruction of the whole sheets as they were originally printed.

Advertising on the backs of stamps did not last long; but two other ways of selling space were quickly developed by governments eager to obtain additional revenues. One way was to print the advertisements on labels attached to stamps; the other was to sell space on covers of postal booklets, on the interleaves, and on labels forming parts of stamp panes inside the booklets.

Postal booklets lend themselves particularly well to advertising since there is a lot of space available and not only can various products be advertised in one booklet but even a coupon can be made from an interleaving sheet or the back cover. Advertising in stamp booklets appears to have originated in Germany in 1906, and its apparently excellent results quickly made this type of advertising very popular. Great Britain, for example, has been a consistent user of this type of advertising and today a wide variety of products and services can be found advertised in their postal booklets.

Other countries which made widespread use of postal booklet advertising are Denmark, Belgium, France, and the various British Colonies. Many American products can be found on these advertisements, particularly automobiles, cameras, tires, and

1

2

3

4

5

6

7

8

9

10

11

12

soaps. A collection of these advertising booklets is a very challenging topic, since they are difficult to come by and require some effort to put together—and they are by no means inexpensive.

Advertising labels attached to stamps were probably first used in Italy in 1924. Advertising labels used with stamps were sometimes made in the form of small labels attached to the stamps at either the top or the bottom, but this caused production problems and the style was abandoned in favor of actual stamp-size labels so that the stamps were simply printed in rows with actual stamps alternating with advertising labels. Normally, the advertising label and the stamp are separated by perforations, but the Italian stamps mentioned above did not have any perforations between the stamps and the advertisements.

A collection of advertising labels with stamps attached is easier to form than a collection of postal booklet advertisements, though it also requires a great deal of search and work to put it together. Generally, it is less costly than collecting booklets.

As was the case with Pears' Soap, many unauthorized examples exist of advertising on stamp booklets and on stamp labels. For example, a French manufacturing chemist, M. Freydier, devised a novel way to advertise his product, *Le Philopode*. He purchased full sheets of stamps at the Post Office and printed his own ads on the margins. He then affixed strips of these to his advertising mailers with the note that they were "offered freely to pharmacists for placing their orders with us." It took a special decree by the French government to halt M. Freydier's productions.

1 and 2. Italian advertising labels of 1924. Fifteen different products were advertised in this manner.

3. Pears' Soap Company's advertisement of 1887, printed on backs of British stamps.

4, 10, 11, and 12. Various pharmaceutical products advertised on small labels attached to French stamps.

5. Commercial advertisement on the cover of a British stamp booklet.

6, 7, and 8. Advertisements printed on the backs of stamps of New Zealand in the 1890s.

9. A German stamp with advertising label attached, both of which have passed through the mail.

2. Agriculture

The importance of agriculture can easily be seen in the number of agriculture-related stamps being issued around the world. The United States Post Office, in particular, has long been issuing stamps for the various facets of this huge industry.

A number of American stamps have been issued directly in honor of various segments of agriculture and agri-business. Others have the theme hidden in the designs—to be "dug out" by the interested collector. The best example of a direct issue is the 1967 commemorative of the centenary of the founding of the National Grange. A good example of a hidden theme is the 1940 Wyoming Statehood commemorative. It depicts the Wyoming State Seal, which lists the state's treasures. Included are the words "grain" and "livestock." The theme is where you find it, which is what makes the hobby challenging, interesting, and educational.

Other direct agricultural stamps include the 1953 stamp for the Future Farmers of America; a stamp issued in 1952 for the 4-H Club movement; the 1959 Soil Conservation Issue, which was a tribute to farmers and ranchers who use soil and water conservation measures; and the 1963 stamp issued for the American "Food for Peace" and "Freedom from Hunger" campaign of the United Nations Food and Agriculture Organization.

There is something for every farmer on American stamps. The fruit grower has the 1966 American Folklore Issue, featuring Johnny Appleseed; the cattle business is represented by a Hereford steer and an ear of corn on the 1967 Nebraska Statehood Commemorative; and a pretty ewe with her lamb decorate the 1971 American Wool Industry Issue commemorating the four hundred and fiftieth anniversary of the introduction of sheep to the North American continent.

These, of course, are only examples, and for most of them there are other stamps to be found that show the theme somewhere in the design. For example, another Hereford steer, several of them, in fact, can be found on the $1 value of the Trans-Mississippi Exposition Issue of 1898, and dairy cattle are shown on a Parcel Post stamp of 1913.

The pleasure of collecting stamps depicting various facets of agriculture can be greatly increased by extending the scope to cover the whole world. Every nation has issued stamps honoring what they consider economically important. Bulgaria honors the cucumber farmer, while Iceland is proud of

7

its tomatoes, and Australia shows beef cattle.

Entire collections can be formed on just one specific aspect of farming. When the poultry industry was honored with an American stamp in 1948 there was a great deal of derision around the country as many city dwellers laughed at the "chicken stamp." But the poultry industry has been widely honored on stamps around the world. Chicken, turkeys, geese, ducks, and eggs have been featured by at least twenty countries on their stamps.

Two other subjects depicted on agriculture stamps are farm equipment and the various methods of farming. Just about every type of farm machine can be found somewhere on a stamp, as can be just about any method of tilling the soil. Modern farm equipment is by far the leading motif on stamps being issued currently. Red China has issued a number of them, and a design featuring a woman tractor driver is a fairly recent issue, one of several depicting women operating modern farm machinery. This is a popular design in many Communist countries. In fact, the tractor is the farm tool most often shown on stamps. The two best tractors on stamps are the stamp of Pakistan which forms part of its set for the twenty-fifth Anniversary of Independence, and the "Opera-

tion Bokassa" stamp issued for its twelfth independence observance by the Central African Republic.

Combines appear on almost as many stamps as do tractors. Poland has issued some interesting stamps along these lines. A Polish-made combine appears on the 1966 issue for the twentieth anniversary of the nationalization of industry, and a striking gold and red stamp depicts the Polish "Bizon" combine harvester.

Combines also appear on stamps of Australia, Canada, Mali, Senegal, and many other nations. Combines for export, an important commodity, have been shown several times on stamps of East Germany. A streamlined unit was used to publicize the 1969 Leipzig Spring Fair. In 1962, stamps showing a combine harvester and a corn picker were issued by East Germany to publicize the Tenth Agriculture Exhibition at Markkleeberg.

Bulgaria issued a long set of stamps in 1967 showing twelve of its agricultural industries. Included in the set is a stamp depicting a modern rose farm, with distilling units shown on the right; another picturing the modern way to raise hops; and one showing the oil mill on a large sunflower farm.

3. Airlines and Civil Aviation

Almost every country in the world has issued stamps honoring civil aviation. The recognition of its importance can be seen by the issuance of stamps in its honor by even the smallest nations—those that can never even hope to have their own flag carriers. Of course, most of the nations that do have flag carriers have issued stamps in their honor.

The United States Postal Service does not identify commercial products and the commercial airplanes shown on its stamps are officially unidentified. Most of these designs are composites, but some have been identified by knowledgeable collectors. The only American stamps that can be related directly to a carrier are the Transpacific air mails of 1935-37, which show Pan Am's "China Clipper" over the Pacific.

Pan American is probably the only United States carrier identified by name on foreign stamps. Pan Am's clipper "John Alden" appears on stamps issued by Liberia in 1957 to commemorate the first anniversary of direct air service between Roberts Field and Idlewild. Another Pan Am aircraft, the "Samoan Clipper," is included in a set issued

by Samoa in 1970 to show the various carriers serving the islands.

The commercial jet most often pictured on a stamp is the Boeing 707, which has appeared on stamps of at least forty countries. The runner up is the Douglas DC-8, which has been shown on stamps by some thirty nations. It holds a record for the number of countries depicting it at one time: On August 31, 1966, all eleven Air Afrique nations issued stamps depicting the DC-8F.

Various other American-made commercial jets are shown on stamps. Several countries have shown the Boeing 720B. The first was Ireland, with a 1961 issue for the twenty-fifth anniversary of Aer Lingus. The two stamps, both identical in design, depict the Dublin airport and two aircraft: the airline's initial De Havilland Dragon and its latest acquisition, the 720B, which was dubbed "Padraig" (St. Patrick).

The Boeing 727 has made it on stamps of several countries. The fiftieth anniversary of Icelandic aviation was honored with a set of two stamps issued September 3, 1969. The 9.50 Krona value depicts the 727; the 12 Krona shows a Rolls-Royce 400. Another

9

good rendition of this jet is on a Colombian Special Delivery airmail of 1966.

The Corvair 880 is on the stamps of China and Ryukyu Islands. The $10 Chinese stamp shown here was issued in 1961 to commemorate the fortieth anniversary of civil air service in Formosa. The 880 shown on the stamp is flying the colors of Civil Air Transport (CAT), the national airline of China, formed in 1946 by the late General Chennault of Flying Tigers fame. China's 880s have been nicknamed the "Mandarin Jets."

Jets, of course, are not the only commercial aircraft shown on stamps. Most countries have issued stamps depicting the older airplanes, particularly in stamp sets issued to mark the anniversaries of flag carriers and air services inaugurations. The Douglas DC-3 of Polynesian Airlines is included in the Samoan set which showed the Pan Am clipper. Another DC-3—one of many on stamps—is included in the 1970 set of St. Vincent, issued to commemorate the twentieth anniversary of regular air services. The set also includes a stamp showing the Grumman Goose amphibian.

A series of stamps issued in 1971 by Monserrat for the fourteenth anniversary of Leeward Islands Air Transport (LIAT) included a Piper Apache and a Beech Twin Bonanza. A 1965 Indonesian stamp depicts a Dakota, and a Sikorsky S-38 and Douglas C-124C Globemaster II appear on the stamps of Antigua.

British commercial jet entries are led by the Hawker Siddeley Comet. It appears on stamps of some twenty countries. Another HS entry, the Trident, was first shown on the stamps of Iraq, issued in 1965 to publicize the Trident jet services of the Iraqi Airways. The BAC VC-10 also has been widely pictured. The stamp shown here is from the set issued by Kenya, Uganda, and Tanzania for the twenty-first anniversary of the East African Airways. Several countries have depicted the BAC 1-11.

The French Caravelle decorates stamps of some twenty nations. Another French entry is the Mystère 20, now known as Fan Jet Falcon. Both France and Great Britain have issued stamps depicting the prime contestant in the race for the airship of the future: the Concorde. The occasion was the first flight of the prototype, March 1, 1969.

A 1956 propeller entry from East Germany marks the opening of passenger service of the German Lufthansa. Two early German air cruisers, the Dornier Wal and the Do-X appear on stamps of Gambia and Antigua.

A postal gallery of civil aviation wouldn't be complete without a showing of Russian airliners. The jets are in first place, and the most popular is the Tupolev TU-104. It's on the stamps of about ten countries.

The fortieth anniversary of Aeroflot, the Russian civil air fleet, was commemorated with a set of stamps issued in 1963. The stamps show an Ilyushin Il-62 and a Tupolev TU-124; the TU-110 exists on a Russian stamp, and the TU-114 is on a stamp of Bulgaria.

Other civil aviation stamps issued for the various flag carriers include many just depicting a symbolic design or the emblem of the carriers; others show their routes. Other civil aviation subjects are airports, airlines' symbols, aviation pioneers, and, of course, a wealth of collateral material such as special cancellations and cachets used on the first day of the stamps' issue or for special flights, souvenir sheets, and postal stationery impressed with stamps.

4. Americana

This chapter is about Americana —anything relating to the United States as portrayed on the stamps of *other nations.*

One would not think that this is a large subject, but the truth is that it is actually a huge subject with thousands of stamps in many collectible categories. Within this enormous subject there is something for any interest: There are American Presidents, the conquest of space, the Statue of Liberty, the flag of the U.S.A., noted American men of science, American-made aircraft, various international organizations in which the United States is a member, World Wars I and II, and the United Nations, to name just a few of the many Americana topics.

Even within these topics there is room for specialization. For example, the topic of American Presidents is very large, for many nations have issued stamps in honor of our various presidents. Hundreds of stamps have been issued around the globe in memory of President John F. Kennedy and many splendid collections have been put together on just this one sub-topic. Some collect foreign tributes to Franklin D. Roosevelt or Abraham Lincoln, both of whom have been honored with a sufficient number of foreign

stamps to allow the building of an interesting collection.

A very large section of Americana is devoted to Americans who have been honored with foreign stamps or whose works have been depicted on foreign stamps. In this category are musicians, movie stars, engineers, athletes, soldiers, inventors, authors, and many others. Many have been identified on the stamp when it was issued; others have been identified later. For example, a stamp of Liberia, issued in 1945, depicted President Roosevelt reviewing troops in Liberia during World War II. The stamp was designed from a photograph, and some years later the photograph was traced and the driver of the President's jeep was identified!

A category opposite the one just mentioned is that of foreigners who became adopted Americans. Here we have such well-known men as Albert Einstein and General Pulaski, and those less widely known, such as, for example, Carl Schurz. Another good example here is the inventor of the linotype, Ottmar Mergenthaler. He was born in Germany in 1854, but emigrated to the United States in 1872. He died in Baltimore in

1899. A related category is one of foreigners who lived, studied, performed, or worked in the United States. This is a large category which includes many foreign presidents who have studied at American universities. There are quite a few artists in this category and many foreigners who made the United States their home after they had to leave, or escape, their native countries.

Another interesting category is that of American products on foreign stamps. We have already mentioned American aircraft (which are on more than one hundred foreign stamps), but there are also American ships, automobiles, motorcycles, weapons, helicopters, and locomotives. Maps showing the location of the United States are a good category, and there are many foreign stamps showing buildings or statues in various American cities. The Statue of Liberty is on a number of foreign stamps, and the United Nations complex in New York City is the world's most widely shown building on stamps.

The telephone, an American invention, is on stamps of at least fifty nations, and American satellites are a common motif of telecommunications-oriented events. Not all American inventions are that widely shown on stamps: the electric bulb appears on only about four.

Two well-known American fraternal orders— Rotary International and the Lions—have appeared on a large number of foreign stamps. The Y.M.C.A., the Red Cross, and the Boy Scouts are also well represented.

Many interesting, out-of-the-ordinary items can be found among Americana. There is a stamp honoring an American who founded the first humane society in Cuba; there is a German stamp depicting a painting which became the basis for the trade mark of an American chocolate manufacturer; there is a Mexican stamp depicting tire tracks made by an American-made tire; there are even stamps made by overprinting advertising labels of an American airplane manufacturer.

The many facets of Americana on stamps of other nations have been described in a large number of articles and in several books. Plenty of material exists to assist the interested collector in building up a prize-winning display of some Americana topic which happens to strike his fancy.

5. Animals

The vast postal world of animals is the second most popular collectible stamp topic in the world. In first place is the conquest of space, but it leads animals only by a very tiny margin. However, if one were to include birds with the animals, it would pass space by far to be the number one topic. (Birds, though animals, are so popular that they are a category by themselves; see Chapter 11.)

The topic of animals is divided into many categories and most people collect those animals in which they have a particular interest. There are simply too many stamps that picture animals for anyone to attempt a collection that would show all of them.

Perhaps the most popular category is that of cats. Cats of all kinds are on a great many stamps, including a recent stamp of the United States, the Mail Order Issue of 1972. The stamp shows a rural post office of old and its "resident" cat is included in the design. Many popular breeds of domestic cats are on stamps and, of course, wild cats are well represented. Cat stamps can be purchased in packets, and packets of animal stamps showing selections of other popular creatures are also available so that one can start a collection very easily.

The horse is also a very popular design and so is horse racing, which is becoming a very popular stamp motif. (Horses and horse racing are described in Chapter 23.)

The dog is a perennial favorite of collectors. The many dog stamps show man's faithful companion in a variety of activities, from hunting to guarding national frontiers. Many of them show sled dogs in the polar regions; there even exist covers of a dog-sled mail which was once tried in Alaska. A great many dog breeds are on stamps and your favorite is almost surely to be found somewhere on postal paper. The popular mongrel is also a well-accepted stamp design—several of these friendly creatures are also on American stamps.

Another extremely popular animal with collectors is the elephant and prize-winning collections have been formed of stamps showing just this one animal. Elephant stamps abound in various interesting designs; many of them very colorful. The elephant is found depicted as a work animal, a royal carrier, a beast of war, and simply as himself. There are also elephants in various coats of arms shown on stamps. Elephant tusks, ivory products, and the elephant's prehistoric ancestors are also depicted and are

often collected together with "regular" elephant stamps.

Fish and other forms of marine life are widely collected and available in vast quantities and in a huge number of designs. Included in this group are sea shells, which can be collected in conjunction with a shell collection, the idea being to show the stamp and the shell which it pictures.

Butterflies and other insects are another large group with many collecting enthusiasts. (They are described in Chapter 25.)

Turtles are an interesting subject for a one-animal collection. There are large numbers of these stamps available and new ones are issued all the time. Other good, and colorful, subjects are snakes and camels. There are even enough stamps around to form a collection of prehistoric and extinct animals.

While some people collect only stamps depicting a certain animal, others form different presentations. Animals have been so well covered by literature that no problem exists in obtaining books and checklists which list them by name (popular and scientific) order, group, and family. Thus, for example, many collect all mammals in their scientific order, while others form collections showing a certain order, or even a certain family of animals. Still others form collections showing geographical distribution of certain species, or collections of animals native to a certain area—state, country, or region.

The vast number of animal stamps allows almost any type of a collection one might fancy. There is enough material for everybody, whether it be for a collection of beasts of burden shown carrying their various cargo, or work animals at their many tasks around the globe.

There are enough animal stamps around to form specific collections relating to one's occupation, if one has anything to do with animals. The dairy industry, the livestock industry—even hog raising—have been formed into interesting and extensive collections. Others along these lines include goat raising, sheep, and poultry.

Besides stamps themselves there also exists a large number of special postal cancellations and cachets showing animals; these are easily found, are generally inexpensive, and can be used in a collection in combination with stamps.

6. Art

In 1974, the general topic of art was the third most popular stamp collecting theme in the world. (This excludes music, which is a general topic by itself, described in Chapter 34.)

Art, of course, is too vast a subject to lend itself to a single collection, though such collections as Indian art, or art of a specific period, do embrace the entire breadth of the subject.

But apart from such collections, most people build theirs around a single art subject. Masks, African wood carvings, stained glass, sculpture, ancient American art, antique furniture, old jewelry, Greek theatre, art galleries, and paintings are some of the subjects which have served as themes for extensive collections.

Artists, too, can be built into collections, and works of art of renowned painters or sculptors have appeared on the stamps of so many nations that they can be sectioned into individual units in a collection. Goya, da Vinci, Rembrandt, Velasquez—these are just some of the names whose works have been widely reproduced on stamps.

Of all the stamps depicting works of art, those reproducing paintings are the most voluminous. Of course, paintings have long been a traditional source of stamp design, but the modern trend is to reproduce paintings on stamps for the sake of showing the painting and not simply to depict the subject of the stamp. Traditionally, for example, the painting of a violin might be used for the design of a stamp issued for a musical event; now, the painting itself would be the subject of the stamp, which would be issued specially to show it as a work of art.

The idea of showing paintings on stamps came from France, which, in 1961, started to issue oversize stamps reproducing the works of French masters. The first set of these stamps included "Blue Nudes" by Matisse, the second set included "Bonjour Monsieur Courbet," and the third set, in 1963, included, besides paintings, reproductions of famous stained glass windows. Each year since, France has issued several such stamps.

The public acceptance of the "paintings stamps" was so enormous that all other postal administrations rushed to display their national treasures on their stamps. Almost all nations have issued stamps depicting paintings and/or stained glass windows. It's safe to state that almost all the world's great paintings have been reproduced on postal

19

paper and hundreds of others—some lesser known works of the masters, others works by national artists important to the issuing country—have been depicted somewhere on stamps.

Sculpture is another good subject for a collection of art, as most of the well-known sculptures are on stamps and more are now appearing as art works gain in popularity as stamp designs. Apparently, the popularity of paintings was a good indication of the popularity of works of art in general.

Ancient jewelry and works of gold and jade have recently appeared on stamps of many nations. Peru, for example, has been issuing sets of stamps depicting ancient jewelry of its various Indian cultures. Taiwan has issued several sets of art on stamps depicting ancient Chinese ceramics and jade, and great art treasures of the Russian Tsars are now regularly appearing on Russian stamps.

Whatever the art subject, someone has probably made it into a stamp collection, or it can be made into one with some effort. Recently, a collection of angels on stamps won a trophy at an Ohio show. Fortunately, there is no shortage of literature on the various art subjects—books, checklists, and articles abound—and the new art stamp issues from various countries are now usually accompanied by detailed information which is reprinted in the philatelic press. Art stamps are easily available in packets of various sizes, with paintings often made up into packets of their own. All this makes art an easily collectible subject within which interesting collections can be built without too much expense.

7. Automobiles

The automobile is not only jamming the highways, it's also starting to crowd postage stamp designs. The rapid spread of the automobile to all corners of the globe is reflected in the growing number of stamps issued with the auto as its focus. While there are probably several hundred stamps with the automobile somewhere in their designs, the "pure" auto stamp—mainly the car—is fairly new, but is already undergoing a transition from merely depicting a vehicle of unidentified parentage to an even "purer" design: an automobile identified by make.

American postal honors for the automobile date back to 1901, when the United States Post Office issued the world's first postage stamp showing an automobile. The stamp forms part of a set issued to commemorate the Pan-American Exposition held that year in Buffalo, New York. The vehicle pictured is a closed-coach electric automobile used in Washington, D.C. by the Baltimore & Ohio Railroad to deliver passengers and baggage.

The automobile as a working tool of the postal service has appeared on United States stamps twice. The first of these stamps is almost unknown to the public, as it formed part of a set issued in 1912 for payment of postage on parcel post packages and it was the only such set of stamps issued in this country (the experiment flopped within one year). The design depicts "automobile service" of the post office. The second stamp was issued in April, 1973, as part of the "Postal People" series.

The automobile has appeared on our stamps on four other occasions: on the commemorative of the fiftieth anniversary of the AAA; on the 1960 "Wheels of Freedom" stamp; on the 1970 Woman Suffrage issue; and on the 1968 stamp issued in honor of Henry Ford. The 1909 Model T, shown in the background of the stamp, is the only auto on United States stamps that has been officially identified by the postal service.

A number of countries have issued stamps for their auto industries, auto shows, and automobile exports. Two very good designs in the industry category come from Poland and both show the manufacture of cars. One is a stamp issued in 1971, showing the construction of a Polish Fiat 125, while the other is a 1971 postal card issued for the twentieth anniversary of the State Auto Works. It also shows a Polish Fiat.

The Twenty-fifth International Automobile Show at Geneva was commemorated with a 1955 stamp of Switzerland. Italy has also is-

sued auto show stamps and Germany has used special commemorative cancellations for such events. A clever design in this category came in 1971 from Belgium, on a stamp issued for the fiftieth Automobile Show at Brussels. The letters of the word "auto" form the shape of a car.

The importance to England of auto exports was shown with the only car stamp ever issued there. It came out in 1966, and it shows a Jaguar and three Mini-Minors. Russia, which has few cars, nevertheless is an active exporter of automobiles and has issued a number of stamps showing its popular export brands. In 1971, an unusual, triangular set of Russian stamps promoted the export of three passenger models: ZAZ-968, Moskvitch-412, and the Volga. Czechoslovakia has also issued a number of auto export stamps, promoting their Skoda vehicles.

During the past few years about 200 different stamps have been issued by over 20 countries depicting a passenger automobile officially identified by make, and often also by year and/or model. American cars hold number one place in this gallery, with at least 23 different makes on some 60 foreign stamps. Many are old makes, no longer manufactured, but new cars are also pictured on stamps.

Though American cars are in the lead in terms of the number of stamps issued that show various makes, the French are not far behind because many of the French-community African nations are issuing many stamps showing earlier French cars. German and Italian cars are on many stamps and the Mercedes-Benz is probably second to the Ford in number of stamps depicting an individual make. The Renault is no doubt in the third place, while Peugeot and Fiat vie for spot number four. The Daimler and the Dion-Bouton have also appeared on a number of attractive stamps.

British passenger autos are also on a number of stamps, with the Rolls-Royce leading the list. There are also many stamps on which the automobile shown has not been identified. The latest arrivals on the postal auto scene are the Japanese, who made their debut in 1972 with a Datsun 240-Z on a stamp of Ajman.

8. Banks and Banking

The first stamp in honor of a bank was issued by Sweden in 1934 to mark the fiftieth anniversary of the foundation of the Swedish Post Office Savings Bank. Since then at least fifty-five countries have depicted bankers and banking on their postage stamps. Postal savings banks have been depicted on stamps of many nations.

The motif of saving is the one most often found on bank stamps. In 1961, Great Britain released three stamps for the centenary of the Post Office Savings Bank. The designs were symbolic pictures of savings. One stamp featured a nut tree, nest, squirrel, and owl. The sixtieth anniversary of the Post Office Savings Bank of Finland was commemorated with a stamp issued in 1947. Postal savings banks have appared on the stamps of Argentina, Belgium, Bulgaria, and many other countries. A set of stamps issued in 1965 by Cameroons to publicize Federal Postal Savings Banks included one showing a savings bank branch and another depicting a piggy bank and coins.

Piggy banks, bees, squirrels, and ants are favorite designs for stamps publicizing savings banks. Another popular design is the passbook. All four motifs have appeared on a set of stamps issued by Poland for the 1961 Saving Month. The fortieth anniversary of Russian savings banks called for two stamps in 1962. Both show a map, a number of savings banks, and a passbook. One of the two also shows depositors.

Various banking anniversaries have been honored with commemorative stamps. The 1950 U.S. commemorative for the seventy-fifth anniversary of the formation of the American Bankers Association is the only American bank stamp. Australia, in 1967, marked 150 years of banking on the continent with a stamp showing old vault keys and a modern vault lock. Various banking meetings have been honored with stamps. In 1943, Argentina issued a stamp for the First National Savings Bank Conference. Another was issued by the Dominican Republic to publicize the Seventh Inter-American Conference for Savings and Loans, Santo Domingo, 1969.

Perhaps the best designs have come from a number of African nations which issued stamps in 1969 for the fifth anniversary of the founding of the African Development Bank. Designers vied with each other for the most striking and unusual design. Rwanda featured reproductions of medieval Flemish paintings depicting bankers and their wives. Burundi issued a souvenir sheet of four stamps depicting how money makes a nation's development possible. Kenya, Uganda, and Tanzania issued a design showing the Euphrobia tree in the shape of the African Development Bank Emblem. Togo showed a hand holding up an industrial complex, and Dahomey featured the horn of plenty. Sierra Leone, Tunisia, and Nigeria also issued stamps for the event.

Another multi-nation bank stamp issue was the 1968 omnibus issue for the fifth anniversary of the West African Monetary Union. Seven former French colonies, now independent nations, issued stamps for the occasion.

National banks of many countries have often been featured on stamps. The one hundred and twenty-fifth anniversary of the National Bank of Greece called for a set of stamps in 1966. The 4 Drachma value shows the Bank's first headquarters. The same year featured bank anniversary stamps from Austria, Norway, and the Philippines. The Bank of Norway was 150 years old and so was the Austrian National Bank, while the Philippine National Bank was just 50. It was also the year of independence for Guyana (formerly British Guiana), which issued a stamp announcing the establishment of the Bank of Guyana. Other anniversary stamps include issues of Argentina, Portugal, Nigeria, Surinam, Sudan, and Turkey.

Turkey has issued several bank stamps. They have depicted their Agricultural Bank, the People's Bank, and the country's cooperative bank, the Security Bank. Probably the oldest bank honored with a stamp is the Bank of Sweden, honored with a stamp on its three-hundredth birthday in 1968.

Postal banks (giros) have been featured by several countries on their postage stamps. Great Britain issued one in 1969. The fiftieth anniversary of post office banking service in Denmark was commemorated with a stamp issued in 1970. Iceland introduced the service in 1971, and issued a stamp to publicize it.

The United Nations have not neglected banking. Their postal issues include a 1960 set in honor of the International Bank for Reconstruction and Development and a 1961 issue for the International Monetary Fund. Austria and Japan have also issued stamps for these organizations.

Bankers, too, have been honored on many stamps. Amadeo P. Giannini, founder of the Bank of America, was honored with a U.S. stamp in 1973. John D. Rockefeller is on a 1955 charity issue of Belgium; the surtax was for anti-tuberculosis work. A 1955 U.S. commemorative honored the centenary of the birth of Andrew W. Mellon.

Jakob Fugger the Rich is on a German commemorative issued in 1959 to mark the five-hundredth anniversary of his birth. Fugger financed kings and popes of his time. In 1519, he established the Fuggerei, a philanthropic foundation still operating. In 1954, Israel issued a stamp for the twentieth anniversary of the death of Baron Edmond de Rothschild of the French branch of the famous banking family, for the many contributions he made to the growth of the State. A Belgian stamp of 1960 was issued in honor of Brother Orban, finance minister in 1948, who played a leading role in the development of the co-operative banks in Belgium. The stamp was for the centenary of the institutions.

9. Basketball

Since the world's first stamp depicting basketball was issued by the Philippines in 1934, some sixty countries have issued over one hundred and fifty stamps featuring basketball in their designs.

Actually, the world's first basketball stamp is American, because the Philippines, in 1934, were a U.S.-administered territory, and with basketball being an American-invented game it was only natural for them to issue the first stamp. In 1961, the United States Post Office issued another basketball stamp, the Naismith-Basketball Commemorative, in honor of the game and to commemorate the centenary of the birth of its inventor, Dr. James A. Naismith.

Basketball stamps have been issued around the globe and, surprisingly enough, it's the Communist-dominated countries of eastern Europe which lead in the number of such stamps. Bulgaria, Czechoslovakia, Hungary, Poland, and Russia have all issued a number of basketball stamps attesting to the popularity of our game. Even Red China has issued two basketball stamps.

Basketball shares with most other team games the difficulty of catching the entire team in a clear grouping, precise and small enough to fit a postage stamp. Thus, most basketball stamps show one, two, or three players involved in some individual fundamental or an element of simple team play.

The simple lay-up shot is the most commonly shown fundamental. Dribbling is not too popular, but overhead shots are seen fairly often, though the form and techniques these paper players often display leaves a lot to be desired. Stamp designers do not seem to be basketball players! Various defensive positions can be seen on stamps, there are some hook shots, and even the jump shot has made its way onto postal paper.

Basketball stamps have been issued as parts of stamp sets depicting popular sports, physical fitness, and particular events. The Third European Basketball Championships, at Kaunas, Lithuania, were honored by a Lithuanian stamp in 1939; Ecuador issued a basketball stamp for the Sixth South American Women's Basketball Championship in 1956; and Panama issued one for the 1938 Fourth Central American Caribbean Games.

Asian countries have issued various basketball stamps for the different sporting

events held in that part of the world. The IV Asian Games in Djakarta, 1962, brought forth a large-size basketball stamp. An unusual triangular stamp with gold borders, depicting a basketball player, was part of the 1969 series by Cook Islands for the Third South Pacific Games at Port Moresby, Papua and New Guinea.

The best known basketball stamp is a Russian commemorative of 1959 inscribed "Victory of the U.S.S.R. Basketball Team— Chile 1959." However, the Third World Championship honors went to Brazil when the Soviet team was disqualified for refusing to play Nationalist China. But, in the eyes of Russia, which did not recognize Nationalist China, they were still champions—and the stamp was issued.

1. United States Naismith-Basketball Commemorative of 1961.
2. World's first basketball stamp, issued by the United States administration of the Philippines for the Tenth Far Eastern Championship Games, 1934.
3. A player executing a left-handed hook on a 1953 stamp of Monaco.
4. Indonesian basketball stamp for the IV Asian Games at Djakarta, 1962.
5. A symbolic basketball stamp, part of a series depicting popular sports, issued in 1963 by Nicaragua.
6. Cook Islands issue for the Third South Pacific Games, 1969.
7. Hungarian basketball issue, part of a set issued to publicize the Sixteenth Olympic Games at Melbourne, 1956.
8. Kuwait depicts basketball game on its 1963 issue for the Arab School Games.
9. Tokyo, 1964 Olympics promotion set of San Marino included this basketball stamp.
10. Ifni, 1958. A basketball stamp promoting physical fitness.

11. A 1966 issue of Rwanda to publicize the National Youth Sports Program.
12. A dribble— seldom seen on basketball stamps— on the Thailand issue for the V Asian Games, Bangkok, 1966.

10. Bicycles and Cycling

The world's postal authorities have often chosen the cycle as a pictorial subject. Many older people may have forgotten the importance of the bicycle, and the younger generation is unaware of the recognition the bicycle has received everywhere, both as a utility vehicle and as a sports machine.

Since the world's first bicycle stamp was issued by Cuba in 1899, almost every country in the world has issued stamps depicting bicycles in their designs. The first bicycle stamps were Special Delivery, and from 1902 until 1922, the United States Post Office used Special Delivery stamps picturing a postal messenger on his bicycle. Many other countries issued similar stamps.

The bicycle was also widely used as a regular mail delivery vehicle. It is still used for that purpose in many countries. A mailman on his bike is shown on a 1967 triangular stamp of Dahomey, and a 1964 stamp of Indonesia shows a bike-mounted postman delivering a letter to a little girl. Bicycle mail delivery is by no means confined to so-called underdeveloped countries. A 1958 stamp of France includes the bicycle as normal means of mail distribution.

The bicycle as a sports vehicle made its first appearance in 1931 on a stamp of Bulgaria issued for the Balkan Olympic Games. This was the beginning of a very popular stamp design. By now, the majority of countries have depicted the sport of cycling on their stamps.

Cycling was an Olympic event from the date the ancient games were revived, in 1896, and many stamps have been issued for Olympic cycling events. The United States stamp, issued in August 1972, is one of many such stamps issued for the Munich Games. In the 1956 Olympiad, the winner of the Road Race, Italian Ercole Baldini, was shown on a triangular stamp of the Dominican Republic. The Dominican Republic was the first country to ever issue stamps showing individual winners of Olympic events, and this is the first identified Olympic cyclist on a stamp. In 1968, in Mexico City, another Italian winner of this event, Pierfranco Vianelli, was shown on a stamp of Fujeira.

A spectacular souvenir sheet from the Arabian sheikdom of Ajman honored the winners of the 2000 meters Tandem event in the 1968 Olympiad, Frenchmen Pierre Trentin and Daniel Morelon. This unusual souvenir sheet is probably the only one of its kind.

The majority of bicycle racing stamps are issued to commemorate various local and international events. A cross-section of these stamps shows various countries and unusual designs. An early bike racing stamp is a 1957 Russian stamp issued for the Tenth Peace Bicycle Race. The cyclists in the stamp have arrived in Warsaw, Poland, which can be identified by the building in the background. Italy has issued many cycling stamps and a modernistic design of a group of cyclists was issued in 1967 for the Fiftieth Bicycle Tour of Italy. Only the front part of the bike is shown on an Italian stamp of 1968, issued to publicize the Bicycling World Championships. It symbolizes track championships at the Velodrome in Rome. The First Bicycle Tour of Java, Indonesia, in 1958, was commemorated with a stamp by Indonesia, while another was issued in 1963 by Monaco for the fiftieth anniversary of the Bicycle Tour de France.

Poland is one of the leaders in number of issued bike stamps. A crowd of racers appears on a 1967 Polish stamp issued for the Twentieth Warsaw-Berlin-Prague Bicycle Race. Called the Peace Race, it is an annual event in Poland. Ten years earlier, another crowd of racers appeared on a stamp of Czechoslovakia issued for the Tenth Peace Race.

Recently, a number of stamps have been issued showing antique cycles. In 1968, an air mail of the Republic of Niger was issued to commemorate the one hundred and fiftieth anniversary of the invention of the bicycle. It shows a modern cycle and an 1818 Hobby Horse, the world's first bicycle. The same year a set of three stamps showing antique bikes was issued by Mali. These are the largest bike stamps issued anywhere. One shows the world's first bike, the Draisienne, or Hobby Horse, invented around 1816 by Baron Von Drais of Germany. The second stamp in the set shows a Michaux bike of 1861. The last stamp of this set is marked "Bicycle 1918," but what the stamp shows is really an English Rover bicycle manufactured about 1875.

A one-of-a-kind bicycle-related stamp is the early air mail issue of Venezuela. It was issued in 1951 to commemorate the Third Bolivarian Athletic Games at Caracas, Venezuela, and its design shows the National Bicycle Racecourse in Caracas.

11. Birds

Birds on stamps are very colorful and very popular with collectors. "Postal" birds have long been among the top 20 topics collected around the world. Bird stamps come in two kinds. One pictures a bird which can be recognized and identified; the other depicts a bird which cannot be placed—perhaps a stylized bird or a symbolic bird or some other artistic rendition of a bird. Generally, only those birds which can be identified are collected.

Since bird stamps have been widely collected for many years, several excellent books exist which list the various stamps and identify them by name. These books have been compiled by professional ornithologists who are also stamp collectors and they make the task of collecting very easy, though there are some differences between the various books because there are differences of opinion between the many bird authorities as to classifications. Also, at times, there is a question as to the proper identification of the bird pictured on a stamp; and, of course, birds on stamps which have eluded classification until now are sometimes identified, adding to the lists.

No one has calculated how many birds are depicted on stamps, but the latest book on the subject, which lists wild birds only, identifies 1063 recognizable species, of which 671 are non-Passerines. The lists identify the birds by orders, families and subfamilies, by common names, and by Latin names. This book does not list domestic birds, but lists of chickens, geese, ducks, and pigeons are available to collectors.

With this many birds on stamps the choice of a specific bird subject is very wide. One may collect scientifically, by order and family, or one can form a collection of a specific family of birds which is appealing. Many collections of individual classes of birds have won prizes at shows. Pigeons on stamps are very popular and there exists a good variety of them. Since pigeons have also been used to carry mail, which they carry strapped to their legs, there also exist "pigeon mail" letters. The dove belongs to the same family as the pigeon and, being the symbol of peace, it is on many stamps. Though the dove is not identified by species, these stamps are also collected by pigeon stamp lovers.

Domestic fowl are on a number of stamps, many of them issued to show native breeds important to the economy of the issuing

BLACK-HEADED GULL 4d

FLAMINGOS BAHAMAS 11c

BRITISH HONDURAS 2c
POSTAGE REVENUE
RED-LEGGED HONEYCREEPER

AUSTRALIA 1854 1954 3½d

CANADA 6

PERDIZ ROJA · ALECTORIS RUFA 5 PTAS CORREOS ESPAÑA

TERRES AUSTRALES ET ANTARCTIQUES FRANÇAISES POSTES RF ARCHIPEL DES CROZET 0.50

ישראל ISRAEL AIR MAIL 0.20

REPUBLIQUE 20c EVEQUE ROUGE RWANDAISE

ACROCEPHALUS ARUNDINACEUS 15 BANI POSTA ROMANA

TIMBRE TAXE REPUBLIQUE ISLAMIQUE DE MAURITANIE POSTES 0F50

WILDLIFE CONSERVATION 8c UNITED STATES CALIFORNIA CONDOR

10 1957

Tristan da Cunha Rockhopper and egg E II R 2½P

WILDLIFE CONSERVATION 8c BROWN PELICAN UNITED STATES

country. These birds are a good subject for a collection. Chickens, for example, are depicted grown, as chicks, and as eggs—there are even stamps showing fried eggs—and such a collection is not difficult to put together.

Other possibilities for bird collections are national birds of different nations, such as the American Bald Eagle, collections of song birds, country collections, and geographic collections. For example, one may want to collect only sea birds. There are many of these on stamps, including the albatross, petrels, pelicans, Frigate birds, cormorants, boobies, gannets, sea eagles, ospreys, skuas, and many kinds of gulls. Also, there is the penguin.

Among the many birds on stamps, the penguin seems to be the favorite. More than half a dozen species of penguins have been pictured by at least a score of nations. There probably exist some 200 stamps depicting these friendly creatures.

The penguin has come to symbolize the "polar aspects" of various stamps issued to publicize polar explorations, geophysical year issues, and research stations both in the Arctic and in the Antarctic. (So solid is the identification of this bird with the cold regions that it is shown also on stamps related to the Arctic issues, despite the fact that it is found only in the Southern Hemisphere.)

The penguin is a favorite design on the Antarctic postal regions, such as the Falkland Islands, South Georgia, and the French and Australian Antarctic Territories. It also appears on a dozen Russian stamps,

issued to honor polar explorations, and on many stamps of other countries issued for "polar" reasons. The emperor penguin and his cousin, the king penguin, appear most frequently. Other penguins on stamps are the Adelie penguin, Gentoo penguin, chinstrap penguin, rockhopper penguin, and the little blue (fairy) penguin.

A very popular collecting topic are American "Duck Stamps"—hunting permit stamps, required under the Migratory Bird Hunting Stamp Act. Although these are not postage stamps, they are sold at post offices, listed in stamp catalogs, sold by stamp dealers, and collected just like stamps. (Anyone may buy them at a post office and they are also for sale by mail at the Philatelic Agency in Washington, D.C.)

Federal Duck Stamps were first issued in 1934. A new stamp is issued each year and a different waterfowl is depicted each time. There are those who regard these stamps as being the most beautiful ever designed. One reason for that is that waterfowl (ducks, geese, and swans) are exceptionally attractive subjects. Another is that some of America's finest wildlife artists have taken part in creating the designs, which are chosen in open competition.

The Fish and Wildlife Service publishes a pamphlet, titled Duck Stamp Data, which contains illustrations of the designs and much interesting information about the stamps and the artists who designed them. The pamphlet may be obtained from the Superintendent of Documents, Washington, D.C. 20402.

12. Chess

The Spassky-Fischer match in Iceland not only brought chess "home" to many people; it also boosted chess on stamps to such popularity that stamps of this subject suddenly became hard to find. There is no doubt that chess on stamps is here to stay as a very popular collectible topic. At the 1974 United States topical show at Rochester, New York, there were two Chess on Stamps exhibits.

Chess first appeared on stamps in Bulgaria, in 1947, when a stamp picturing a chess piece—the Knight—was included in a set of sports stamps issued for the Balkan Games. (The Knight seems to be the favorite piece to be shown on stamps; the Rook is in second place.)

These days, the chess stamp is no longer to be found as part of sports sets—it now stands on its own, with strikingly designed singles and sets issued specifically for chess-related events. Since Bulgaria's inauguration of the motif, at least 25 countries have issued stamps pertaining in one way or another to chess. Together, these countries have produced some 40 sets of stamps, totalling some 100 values.

Since chess is very popular in Eastern Europe it is not surprising that those nations lead in the number of chess stamps issued and in the variety of designs. Bulgaria issued a chess stamp again in 1958, to commemorate the Fifth World Students' Chess Games at Varna, and in 1962 it issued a set of five stamps and a souvenir sheet to commemorate the Fifteenth Chess Olympics, also at Varna.

Perhaps the best-designed set of chess stamps so far are the five stamps issued in 1950 by Jugoslavia to publicize the International Chess Matches at Dubrovnik. Two of the stamps show flags of competing nations.

As might be expected, Russia leads in the number of chess stamps— at least 11, issued on several different occasions. The first Russian chess stamps were issued in 1948—a set of three to publicize the Sixteenth Chess Championship for world leadership. Other Russian chess stamps have been issued to commemorate the fiftieth anniversary of the death of the Russian chess player, M. I. Chigorin; to publicize the Thirtieth Russian Chess Championships; to commemorate the Twenty-fifth Championship Chess Match, Moscow, 1963; and to commemorate the world title chess match between Tigran Petrosyan and Boris Spassky.

East Germany has also issued several chess stamps, including three in 1960 for the Fourteenth Chess Championships at Leipzig, and a single in 1969 to publicize the Sixteenth Students' Chess World Championships in Dresden. Poland, Romania, and Hungary have all issued chess stamps. The Romanian set of six stamps showing different chess pieces was issued in 1966 for the Chess Olympic in Cuba.

Cuba issued several chess stamps in 1951 to commemorate the thirtieth anniversary of the winning of the world chess title by José Raoul Capablanca. One of these stamps shows the chess board as it was at the resignation of Dr. Lasker, and another pictures Capablanca making "The Exact Play." The only other chess stamps from the Western Hemisphere are from Nicaragua and the Dominican Republic, where they were issued in 1967 to commemorate the Fifth Central American Chess Championships at Santo Domingo.

The Spassky-Fischer match was commemorated with a 1972 stamp of Iceland, showing a map of Iceland superimposed on a chess board. Other European chess stamps have been issued by France, Finland, Spain, Monaco, San Marino, and West Germany.

Other nations issuing chess stamps include Israel, which issued a set of three values in 1964 to commemorate the Sixteenth Chess Olympics at Tel-Aviv; the Netherland Antilles, which commemorated the 1962 International Candidates Chess Tournament at Willemstaad with a set of three stamps; and the Philippines, which issued a stamp in 1962 depicting José Rizal playing chess. Other chess stamps have come from the State of Oman, Yemen, and the Trucial States sheikdom of Fujeira.

A collection of chess stamps can also include the many special cancellations which were issued by the post offices of the nations which issued stamps for chess-related events. First day covers also exist for most chess stamps, and in many cases there are several cachets for a single issue. There also exist what is called by collectors "maximum cards," which are postcards or photos with pictures identical with the design of a stamp (or part of the design) to which the stamp is affixed and cancelled, usually with a special commemorative cancellation.

13. Christmas

In 1971, an incredible 1.2 *billion* copies of a single postage stamp were printed by the United States Postal Service. It was the largest stamp printing order in the world since postage stamps were first introduced in 1840. It was almost ten times larger than the usual printing of an American commemorative stamp.

The stamp was one of two Christmas stamps issued that year. It depicted a nativity scene by the Italian painter Giorgio Giorgione, "Adoration of the Shepherd," and portrayed five figures— Mary, Joseph, the Christ Child, and two shepherds. (The original painting, done about 1510, is in the National Art Gallery in Washington.)

The enormous demand for this stamp shows not only the great popularity of Christmas stamps but also points out the demand for stamps that directly reflect the Christian significance of the holiday. The other Christmas stamp issued that year featured a "popular" Christmas design, "A Partridge in a Pear Tree," and its sales were far below the sales of the Giorgione design.

Christmas stamps are a fairly new idea. Because "XMAS 1898" appears in the design of 2¢ stamps issued by Canada 75 years ago, they are popularly regarded as the first Christmas stamps. This claim to fame is doubtful because they were issued to commemorate a secular event, the introduction of the Imperial Penny Postage scheme on Christmas Day, 1898. The Canadian post office never thought that they might be used on holiday greetings.

The first stamp intended to be used on Christmas greetings was issued by Austria in 1937. Its motif was a rose, a Christmas design peculiar to that country. In fact, for the first thirty years of their use, Christmas stamps around the world tended to be motifs. Some nations showed universally accepted Christmas motifs, a star, for example, while others displayed what is special to each country: the United States has shown a poinsettia; Austria, as we have seen, a rose. Others yet showed the joy of children, their toys, the tree decorations, the various ways of St. Nicholas— or Santa Claus, or Father Christmas. It's hard to think of a Christmas motif that has been omitted from stamps. Even "Silent Night, Holy Night" found its way on a stamp when Austria issued one to commemorate the hymn's one hundred and thirtieth anniversary in 1948.

The first Christmas stamp to portray a part of the story of the birth of Christ was issued

by Brazil in 1939— 99 years after the issuance of the world's first postage stamp. It shows the Three Wise Men and the Star of Bethlehem. The first full set of stamps to show nothing but the story of Christmas appeared in Hungary in 1943. Over the next 15 years Christmas stamps appeared sporadically with very few new countries joining those already issuing them.

The number of Christmas stamp-issuing nations slowly started to grow in the 1958-1961 period. During those four years Costa Rica, Spain, New Zealand, Norfolk Island, Peru, and several others joined the Christmas stamp club. The designs also underwent a change and the Christmas story largely replaced the motifs. In 1959 appeared the first set of Christmas stamps from the Vatican, three beautiful reproductions of the "Nativity," by Raphael.

The issuance of a Christmas stamp by the United States in 1962 no doubt helped to popularize the idea. This first American stamp offering was a small, modest green and red stamp showing a Christmas wreath and candles. It cost four cents then to send a letter. That stamp caused a lot of controversy, with many people objecting to it on the grounds that the government was mixing business with religion, but its acceptance was so overwhelming that the critics simply disappeared. Since that year, the United States has issued Christmas stamps annually, and several times has offered more than just one. Four were issued in 1964, and five in 1970.

In 1964, Canada issued its first "real" Christmas stamp and it turned out to be so popular that within six years she was issuing a dozen different Christmas designs. By 1966, when 22 countries issued Christmas stamps (including Great Britain), it was clear that the Christmas stamp was here to stay.

By 1968, the list of issuing countries grew to 44, and since 1970 some 50 nations have annually issued stamps recalling the birth of Christ. The designs of the Christmas stamps are now predominantly religious, with much emphasis placed on reproductions of paintings by old masters and on ancient stained glass windows. The nativity scene has been very popular and has appeared on stamps of Spain, Antigua, New Zealand, Great Britain, Australia, and many other countries.

Another popular design is the Three Kings. They have appeared on stamps from all corners of the globe; some designs have been traditional, others modern. The two extremes can be seen in 1971 issues of Great Britain and New Zealand. The British set depicted the Wise Men as shown in the three upper panels of a window in the North Choir Aisle of Canterbury Cathedral. These stained glass windows are about eight hundred years old and it seems miraculous that they have survived eight centuries, including the bombings of World War II. At the other end of the world, the New Zealand design was a symbolic Three Kings, by the contemporary artist Enid Hunter. Enid is a telephone operator who paints in her spare time.

Christmas stamps have been issued by countries from which they would hardly be expected. Jordan has issued one, and so has Korea. The Arabian sheikdoms of Trucial States have poured out a veritable deluge of Christmas stamps in magnificent designs, but they were strictly a money-making deal for those governments: "export" products that never saw any postal service in their native countries. Egypt has issued "greeting card" stamps in December during various years. They show different motifs— in 1969 it was the American poinsettia.

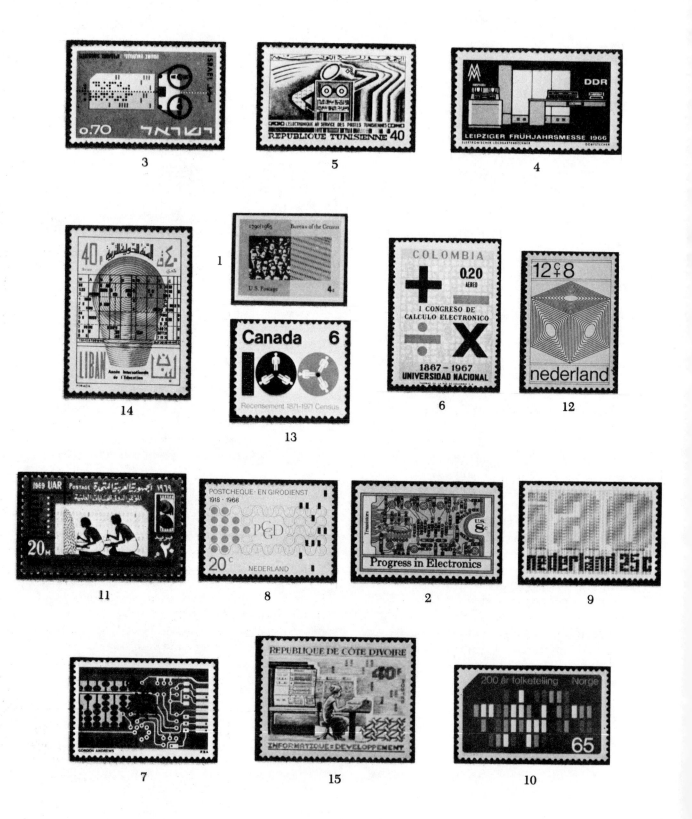

14. Computers and EDP

Only a handful of stamps picture EDP paraphernalia as part of the design, most of them having been issued since 1969, but the design is rapidly gaining in popularity.

There are a number of stamps depicting automation in various applications—mostly manufacture and communications—but they do not show any EDP equipment, though it is obvious that without it the automation processes shown would not exist.

"True" EDP stamps, those directly related to the computers or depicting some aspect of EDP in their designs, number only about 30. They have been issued by some 20 countries on at least 22 different occasions. The United States, where the modern computer was invented, has not yet issued a "computer" stamp, but in 1965, it did issue a postal card featuring a punched card (1). Also, a printed circuit board assembly appears on one of its "Progress in Electronics" stamps, issued in 1973 (2).

The first computer stamp was issued in 1964 (3) as part of a set issued to publicize Israel's contributions to science. In 1966, a computer appeared on an East German stamp issued in February to publicize the 1966 Leipzig Spring Fair (4). Later that year,

a space conquest set of Czechoslovakia included a stamp showing the binary code.

Russia entered computer philately in 1967 with a stamp issued to commemorate industrial progress. "Computer tape" is included in the official description of the design.

Nineteen sixty-eight saw several computer stamps issued. A "humanized" computer appeared on three Tunisian stamps issued to publicize the introduction of electronic equipment into the postal service (5). Colombia issued an air mail to commemorate the First Data Processing Congress in 1967 held in conjunction with the centenary of the National University (6). The official designation of the design is "computer symbols." The 1968 Australian set issued to commemorate the Ninth International Congress of Soil Science includes a stamp whose design represents "soil testing through chemistry and by computer." Another Australian computer stamp issued that year formed part of a set issued to publicize the use of satellites for weather observations and communications. Magnetic tape reels appear within the design. Australia's third postal computer entry came in 1972 with a design comprising an abacus, numerals, and computer circuits. The stamp was issued for the Tenth International Congress of Accountants (7).

Punched cards on stamps first appeared in 1968, from The Netherlands, the leader in number of computer stamps issued (8). It was issued to commemorate the fiftieth anniversary of the postal checking service. In 1971, The Netherlands issued another punched card stamp, to commemorate the fourteenth national census. In 1969, The Netherlands issued two stamps to commemorate the fiftieth anniversary of the International Labor Organization. The design, produced by a line printer, is made up of 28 minute lines, each reading "1919 internationale arbeidsorganisatie 1969" (9).

Norway issued a stamp with a punched card in 1969 (10) to commemorate the two hundredth anniversary of the first Norwegian census. The 1969 UAR (Egypt) issue to publicize the International Congress for Scientific Accounting, Cairo, was a stamp depicting ancient arithmetic and a computer card (11). A CRT display was included in a stamp issued that year by Trinidad and Tobago.

In 1970, Switzerland showed an OCR form on a stamp issued for the Federal Census of 1970; Thailand showed a punched card on its census stamp; Romania issued a "computer art" souvenir sheet for EXPO '71, and Mexico had two stamps showing an electrostatic dot printing matrix. Also, from The Netherlands came a set of six stamps showing various designs made by a computer: isometric projection from circle to square (12), parallel planes in a cube, two overlapping scales, transition phases of concentric circles with increasing diameters, four spirals.

In 1971, Canada issued a census commemorative depicting five-level paper tape and magnetic drives (13); Poland honored the Sixth Congress of Polish Technicians with a stamp depicting computer tape; Lebanon issued two air mails (same designs but different values and colors) depicting punched cards as its commemoratives of the International Education Year (14), and Cuba showed magnetic tape drive.

The Ivory Coast issued a computer stamp in 1972 (15), and a computer control console for Apollo XII Moon Mission appeared on a 1972 stamp of Ras al Khaima.

Other computer-related stamps include those issued in honor of personalities associated with its history and development and the several issued since the United States' entry of 1973.

15. Construction Industry

The importance of the construction industry can be easily seen by a glance at the gallery of stamps issued in its honor and in the commemoration of major construction projects by almost all nations. Just about every country has issued stamps either honoring the industry or its works.

The American entry in the gallery of direct honors is the 1952 commemorative of the centenary of the founding of the American Society of Civil Engineers. Russia has issued a number of stamps for the construction industry. Two of them are shown here; the tall stamp, one out of a set issued in 1956 in honor of Builders' Day, depicts buildings under construction. The horizontal stamp was issued in 1965 and shows "New materials for building industry." The Eastern nations are prolific issuers of construction stamps. China, Bulgaria, Albania, East Germany, and Hungary have all issued a number of them. A striking red and gold construction stamp was included in the 1971 series issued by Poland for the Sixth Congress of the Polish United Worker's Party.

France honored the industry with a stamp issued in 1957, depicting "the public works of France." Venezuela included a stamp showing a crane and building construction in its 1964 series to commemorate the centenary of the Department of Industrial Development. Viet Nam has issued a large number of construction stamps. The one shown here forms part of a set issued to publicize rural construction.

An imaginative, one-of-a-kind design was used by Belgium in 1969 for the fiftieth anniversary of the International Labor Organization. It reproduces a painting by F. Leger, "Construction Workers." One of the best designs is the 1971 modern, bold design of Lesotho, typical of the new designs being issued by the emerging nations.

The emerging nations, proud of their modern facilities, provide the best designs for stamps showing projects under construction. The industrialized nations prefer to show the works completed. A large spectacular issued in 1969 by Abu Dhabi shows buildings under construction for the Abu Dhabi Airport. On the other end of the scale, the laying of urban water pipes was sufficiently important in Senegal to warrant a stamp depicting the operation. Construction of pipelines and waterworks has been shown

on various stamps. One of the few major nations to show works in progress is the People's Republic of China. The stamp shown here, issued in 1964, shows the construction of the Hsin An Kiang Dam.

Dams and bridges appear on stamps of almost all nations which have them, and many of the more famous ones have been pictured by several countries. Recently, another major construction project—an airport—has been added to the list of the "must" designs. The U. S. has not depicted any of its airports on stamps, but most other nations have shown them, including Russia, China, and France.

The United States has issued stamps showing a number of its bridges. New York's George Washington Bridge is on the A.S.C.E. stamp mentioned earlier. The Niagara Railway Suspension Bridge appeared on a stamp in 1948 and the opening of the Verrazano-Narrows Bridge called for a commemorative in 1964. The same year, Italy issued a stamp in honor of Giovanni da Verrazano (discoverer of New York Bay) showing the bridge that bears his name and his portrait. In 1971, British Honduras issued a set of stamps depicting world-famous bridges, in which one stamp shows the "Narrows Bridge." Another stamp of this set depicts the London Bridge, before and after its "transplantation" to Arizona.

Britain has issued stamps showing some of her old bridges, and in 1964 a new bridge stamp appeared to commemorate the opening of the Forth Road Bridge in Scotland. The Sydney Harbor Bridge is on a stamp of Australia.

A very recent addition to the huge gallery of dams on stamps is the South African set of 1972 issued for the inauguration of the Hendrik F. Verwoerd Dam of the Orange River Project. Both the Grand Coulee and the Boulder Dam appear on stamps of the United States. The Donzère-Mondragon Dam is on a stamp of France; the irrigation dam at Djorf Torba-Oued Guir is on a stamp of Algeria, while Turkey shows the Keban Dam.

It's difficult to think of any type of heavy construction which does not appear on stamps. Tunnels are a popular design and a number of nations have issued stamps showing them. The stamp shown here, issued in 1969 by Argentina, shows the tunnel under the Rio Grande from Santa Fe to Parana. Subways are being built all over the world, and their construction is usually shown on stamps. Russia has issued perhaps twenty stamps showing the construction and finished stations of the Moscow subway system. Hungary commemorated the opening of the Budapest "Metro" with a stamp in 1970. A modern pipeline and a pumping station are on a 1957 stamp of Iraq. The Mustola Lock appears on the Finnish stamp of 1968, issued for the opening of the Saima Canal—one of a number of stamps showing man-made waterways. The Panama Canal, of course, appears on many United States stamps issued for use in the Canal Zone. A set of 16 stamps, issued in 1939, depicts the complete construction of the Canal.

Major national construction projects are often publicized on stamps. Australia's Snowy Mountain Scheme was publicized with a set of stamps issued in 1970, one of which is shown here. The Dutch Delta Plan, was publicized in 1972 by a stamp of The Netherlands, showing a map of the Delta.

16. Dentistry

There is quite a bit of philatelic material available to the dentist who might want to try to form a collection. At least forty countries have issued stamps directly related to dentistry.

The American 4-center issued in 1959 to commemorate the centenary of the American Dental Association is only one in a goodly gallery of United States dental stamps.

The first American dental personality honored on a stamp is Benjamin Rush, one of the physicians who signed the Declaration of Independence. He related oral and systemic disease, spoke of carious teeth, and recommended extraction to cure general diseases. He is shown on a 1969 stamp depicting the "Signers of the Declaration of Independence," by Trumbull.

George Eastman appears on a 1954 stamp. He established the first dental clinic in the world for children, the Eastman Dental Dispensary, in 1918.

A 2-cent stamp in the 1940 series of Famous Americans honors Dr. Crawfold Williamson Long of Jefferson, Georgia. Dr. Long demonstrated ether anesthesia after seeing it used by Dr. W. T. G. Morton. He, in turn, is said to have learned about it from a dentist at Hartford, Connecticut, a Dr.

Horace Wells. Wells himself had a tooth extracted under the influence of the "laughing gas" and had thereafter used it in his practice. There is still controversy over who discovered it.

Paul Revere is on a 25-cent stamp of the Liberty Series of 1954-1968. Revere was only a casual dentist, with about six years of sporadic activity. In 1776, Revere identified the body of Joseph Warren by a dental appliance. It was the first case in America of identification by means of teeth.

The ancient practitioners are the ones most often honored on stamps. Many countries have thus honored the Arabian physician Avicenna (980-1037). He wrote three treatises on dentistry. He believed that toothache was caused by worms which chewed away dental substance. For pulpitis, he drilled into the tooth and introduced certain remedies into it. To relieve pain, he severed the nerve by shaking the aching tooth with forceps.

Rabbi Moses Maimonides has been honored by several countries. Theologist, philosopher, and physician, he became the doctor of Sultan Saladin in spite of his Hebrew origin. He wrote about the treatment of toothache, extraction, halitosis, and toothbrushing. He noted that a broken tooth could be restored with a gold shell crown.

The "Father of Medicine," Hippocrates, has also been honored widely. He discovered that the development of teeth begins before birth and that, after the first teeth are shed, permanent teeth are formed "by food and drink." He was the first to recommend the use of dentrifices. He invented a number of dental instruments, including a crude dental forceps.

Others honored include another Arabian physician, Albucasius, who lived from 936-1013. He was interested in the care of the teeth and recommended thorough cleansing of the teeth and removal of tartar. He made artificial teeth from ox bone and illustrated a set of 14 scrapers and scalers in his *De Chirugia*.

Another old-timer depicted is Rhazes, also known as Abu Bakr Muhammad ibn Zakariyya Ar Razi, born in Persia around 1100 years ago. He was a musician, philosopher, and physician and was honored by a set of stamps of Persia in 1964. He was the first man to fill teeth in order to preserve them; he used extraction only as the last resort. His attempt to arrest tooth decay was a cement of mastic and alum.

A French stamp issued in 1961 honors Pierre Fauchard, the "Father of Dentistry." He was responsible for the definite separation between medicine and dentistry. Technical literature on dentistry began with his *Chirugien Dentiste* (1728). He used human teeth and artificial teeth made from hippopotamus tusks, ivory, and ox bone, maintained them in place with linen, silk, or gold thread passing through various holes made in them and tied to natural teeth. His full dentures had uppers and lowers attached to each other by metal springs.

Others honored on stamps include another believer in worms, the famous French surgeon Ambroise Pare. He thought that caries was caused by worms. The list of personalities includes Johann Wolfgang von Goethe, discoverer (in 1786) of os incisivum; Andreas Vesalius, who described the pulp cavity; Roentgen and Lister; Ivan P. Pavlov, the Russian, whose work on the activities of the salivary glands is of great importance to the dental practitioner; Leonardo da Vinci, who made the first accurate drawings of the teeth; Johannes E. R. von Purinje (Czechoslovakia), who created the term "Dentin," and many others.

The visible practice of dentistry includes a stamp of Qatar which shows a dentist attending a patient in the chair, and another, of similar nature, issued by St. Helena. A series of stamps issued in 1964 by Papua and New Guinea includes one showing a dentist treating a schoolchild patient.

Toothbrushes have made it on stamps. A Hungarian stamp of 1963 pictures a child with a towel and toothbrush. A Netherlands stamp showed a girl brushing her teeth in 1954, and another child with a toothbrush is on the 1971 New Zealand issue for the Golden Jubilee of the School Dental Service.

Dental associations and congresses have been honored with stamps. Bulgaria issued a stamp in 1969 to publicize the fifth annual session of the International Dental Federation; Korea issued a stamp to honor the Fifth Asian Pacific Dental Congress, and Iran issued stamps in 1964 and 1965 to honor the meetings of the Iranian Dentists' Association's Congresses.

Various related materials are available to the dental philatelist: Commemorative postmarks for dental meetings; dental health slogan cancellations; stamps showing skulls—with teeth showing, and many others.

17. Electric Power Industry

Almost every country in the world has honored the electrical industry on its stamps. There are thousands of stamps depicting in their designs some facet or another of this vital industry.

The pioneers in electric inventions and their machines have been honored by stamps of many nations, the early uses of electricity have been depicted, and many sets of stamps have been issued to commemorate and publicize electrification programs in various countries. The electric power industry itself has been the object of many commemorative issues. Hydroelectric power stations and municipal power plants have been depicted on a number of stamps and recently this motif has been extended to include nuclear power centers. The myriad manufactures and industries depending on electricity are depicted on stamps of all nations.

Stamps have been issued which show transformers, high voltage lines, electronic equipment, radios and TVs, telephones and telegraphs, home appliances, turbines, and many other kinds of useful tools. At least four stamps exist depicting the lowly light bulb—lowly only if you have it; many people around the globe still have to make do with candles.

It's difficult to think of a power application that has not been featured on a stamp. A collection of such "electricity" stamps could be put together to show a complete history of the industry and the many uses of electricity—the power that moves the world of the twentieth century.

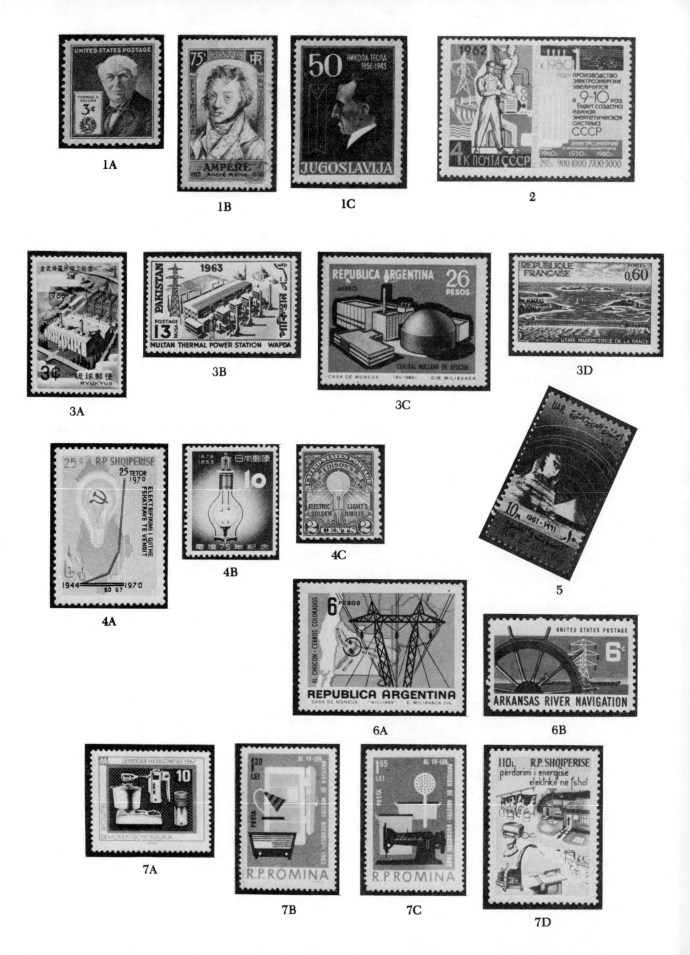

1A

1B

1C

2

3A

3B

3C

3D

4A

4B

4C

5

6A

6B

7A

7B

7C

7D

1. Some of the inventors who made it all possible: (From left to right) United States stamp of 1947, issued to commemorate the centenary of the birth of Thomas Alva Edison. The man who gave us the amp, André Marie Ampère, was honored with a stamp of France, issued in 1936. Several countries have issued stamps in honor of Nikola Tesla. The one shown here was issued by Yugoslavia in 1956.

2. One of many stamps to honor the electric power industry, this large spectacular is a Russian issue of 1962.

3. Many stamps honoring the electric power industry feature power stations. Others feature power stations on issues depicting progress. The first stamp on the left, a 1965 issue of Ryukyu Islands, features the Kin power plant. Next to it is a stamp of Pakistan issued in 1963 to commemorate the opening of the Multan Thermal Power Plant. The next stamp depicts the Atucha Nuclear Center depicted on a 1969 air mail of Argentina. The last stamp shows the French Rance Power Station which uses tidal water to generate electricity.

4. The electric bulb has not been omitted from stampic honors. On the left, it is shown on a stamp of Albania, where until recently it wasn't at all common. This 1970 stamp was issued to publicize the completion of village electrification. The stamp in the center depicts the first electric lamp in Japan. It was issued in 1953 to commemorate the seventy-fifth anniversary of electric lighting in Japan. On the right is the Electric Light Jubilee Issue of 1929. The stamp features Edison's first lamp, invented October 21, 1879.

5. The Sphinx at night. Illuminated for the tourists— by electricity, of course. It's only since 1961 that the Sphinx and the Pyramids have been lit up at night by electricity; for the five thousand years preceding that event (commemorated by this stamp of Egypt) the only illumination available was the light of the moon and the stars.

6. High voltage lines strung from the power stations to the city are not solely an American attraction. They're everywhere— everywhere people are fortunate enough to have electric power. The ones on the stamp on the left are in Argentina. On the right is the 1968 Arkansas River Navigation commemorative issued for the opening of the Arkansas River to commercial navigation.

7. Unusual and unique, these four stamps are probably the world's only stamps showing electrical household appliances. The first is from East Germany, the pair in the center is from Romania, and the last one is from Albania.

18. Flowers

Stamps picturing flowers are one of the most popular categories in topical collecting. It's an area of collecting particularly favored by the feminine collector. More than 3000 stamp designs feature flowers or plants.

Switzerland was the first country to bring the beauty of a flower to a postage stamp, and the first to realize the publicity value of picturing native flowers in full color on stamps. For many years Switzerland issued a yearly colorful series showing its flowers—edelweiss, alpine rose, slipper orchids, and many others. Moderately priced then, and still so, they rapidly found their way into special collections.

Inspired by the Swiss success, other nations followed suit, until now almost every country that issues stamps has honored flowers on some of them. The many American flower stamps include several statehood commemoratives showing state flowers. A magnolia was on the Mississippi Statehood Commemorative. A sunflower appeared on the Kansas Statehood stamp. Flowers of the giant saguaro cactus were on the issue observing Arizona's fiftieth anniversary of statehood. In 1958, the Garden Clubs of America were honored with a three-cent commemorative stamp, now known as the Gardening-Horticulture Issue. It depicts "Bountiful Earth," and its issuance came on the centenary of the birth of the renowned American horticulturist Liberty Hyde Bailey.

Another American flower stamp of note was the Moina Michael Issue of 1948, depicting her and three poppies. (Moina Michael was the originator of the Flanders Field Poppy Day as a memorial to war dead.) The 1964 Christmas stamps, an issue using four designs, included one depicting the poinsettia, a genuinely American Christmas flower. In other parts of the world different flowers serve as symbols of the holidays. In Austria, for example, the rose is symbolic of Christmas—an Austrian rose stamp of 1937 was the first stamp specifically intended for holiday greetings.

Other United States stamps in this category include two of the quartet issued in 1969 for the Eleventh International Botanical Congress at Seattle. The flora of the Northeastern United States was depicted by a lady's slipper orchid; the Southeast was represented by the flower of Franklinia. Our most striking flower stamps were the four issued in 1969 to publicize natural beauty. To stamp collectors these are known as the

Beautification of America Issue. They picture a medley of common but beautiful flowers—azaleas, tulips, daffodils, poppies, lupines, and crab apple blossoms.

Probably more stamps picture orchids than any other flowers, for tropical nations have produced several hundred colorful stamps depicting these exotic blossoms. Roses have been depicted frequently, a recent addition being a striking set of three stamps issued by New Zealand for the 1971 World Rose Convention. Orchids and roses are the two most popular flowers for stamps, but almost any flower you can think of has appeared somewhere on a stamp.

The large variety of stamps with floral designs gives the collector almost unlimited scope in the development of his collection. He can seek stamps showing the flowers of a particular area or even a country. He can collect stamps showing certain flowers or families of flowers. He may decide to collect stamps picturing exotic species or familiar ones. All will be stamps of great appeal to the eye and even a modest collection will be something he can show with pride.

19. Gems and Minerals

With the issuance of the four American Mineral Heritage stamps, on June 13, 1974, the United States joined a long list of nations which have issued stamps depicting their mineral treasures.

Gems and minerals on stamps are a very popular collecting topic because there are many ways of relating the "paper minerals" to the "rocks." Some collectors seek out stamps showing minerals in their natural state. Others include cut gems, and still others collect native metals and ornamental stones which are not in their natural state. Some collect mining stamps and stamps showing jewelry, but the number of stamps showing cut gems is untold and a complete collection is rather impractical.

A very interesting way of relating the stamps to the minerals is a combination collection consisting of mineral specimens and stamps depicting them. The ideal goal here is to obtain minerals from the country issuing the postage stamp. A drawback is the cost of some of the specimens, such as, for example, raspberry-colored fluorite crystals on stamps of Switzerland, not to mention such pretties as diamonds or emeralds.

However, facet replicas are a reasonable solution where the original is too costly.

Most minerals useful in commerce have been depicted on stamps, and so have the procedures for mining them. These include gold, silver, copper, lead, asbestos, tin, sulphur, coal, gypsum, uranium, manganese, salt, nickel, galena, phosphates, platinum, etc. Many countries have issued stamps depicting gold prospecting. The United States Post Office issued a stamp in 1959 to commemorate the centenary of the discovery of silver at the Comstock Lode, Nevada. Prior to the issuance of the Mineral Heritage stamps, these were the only United States entries in the paper gallery of gems and minerals.

Four new American stamps depict amethyst, rhodochrosite, tourmaline, and petrified wood cut and polished as gems. The stamps showing rhodochrosite and petrified wood are probably the first such designs to be issued anywhere. Amethyst has also been pictured on stamps of East Germany, Russia, Switzerland, Uruguay, and Botswana. Tourmaline appears on stamps of South-West Africa and Switzerland. Other gemstones

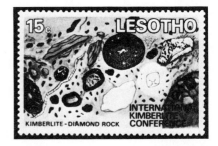

shown on stamps include diamonds, topaz, rhodonite, rubies, sapphires, emeralds, zircon, helidor, opals, lazulite, agate, smoky quartz, garnet, rock crystal, jasper, and malachite. Carved jade appears on the stamps of many countries, as do fossils. Both these subjects are becoming popular, particularly the fossils because more countries can show them than can show jade.

Stamps showing pearls also exist.

One can learn something from studying the background of the gems that are pictured on stamps. For example, in 1973, Australia issued four gem stamps. By looking up the gems depicted we learn that the chrysoprase shown on one of the stamps is an apple-green variety of chalcedony, used as a gem. The color is caused by the presence of nickel oxide. Its name is from the Greek, which means "golden leek." The second stamp depicts agate. The next shows an opal, a popular Australian gem. Opal is not a crystal, but a sort of solidified jelly. Before the discovery of opal fields in New South Wales and Queensland in Australia, opals came mainly from Cervenica, near Kosice in Czechoslovakia. The last stamp pictures rhodonite, another gemstone with greek in its name—rhodon, meaning a rose.

As may be expected, the diamond is the gem most often shown on stamps. Gems, miners, and collateral materials have appeared on a number of stamps. The "home" of the diamond industry, South Africa, has issued only one diamond stamp, but it is the only design consisting of nothing but the cut stone. Another large cut stone is on a stamp of the Ivory Coast, which also shows a diamond mine. The third large cut stone is on a 1968 stamp of Israel. Another stamp in this Israel set depicts what appears to be a diamond necklace with an emerald.

A diamond accompanied by drops of water appears on a stamp of France, issued in 1969 to mark the European Water Charter. Five gem diamonds are on a 1974 stamp of Botswana. Another five-diamond stamp of Botswana was issued in 1970, to publicize "Developing Botswana." The stamp also shows the Orapa diamond mine. Another stamp of this set pictures the Orapa diamond treatment plant.

The best diamond mining set so far came in 1973 from Botswana's neighbor, Lesotho. The four stamps were issued to publicize the International Kimberlite Conference in Lesotho, and depict in detail the process of the forming of diamonds and the mining procedure. (Kimberlite is the name of a rock of volcanic origin from which diamonds are derived.) It is a very interesting set of stamps.

Diamond mines and miners are also on stamps of Sierra Leone, Central African Republic (a diamond grader), and Tanganyika. There are also diamonds on stamps of Ghana, South-West Africa, Angola, Belgium, Congo, Andorra, Russia, and Sierra Leone.

20. Golf

Just about every sport in the world has been depicted on a postage stamp, and the game of golf is no exception. Though it is something of a late-comer to the world of stamps, the past five years have seen the design used by several countries. This is a good indication that more golf stamps are certain to appear in the future, because once a stamp is found acceptable by several countries, others quickly follow suit.

The first golf-related stamp is the 1953 Japanese pictorial out of a series depicting their national parks. The design depicts a view of "Mt. Unzen from the golf course." A portion of the golf course is visible on the stamp (1). Next is a stamp from French West Africa issued in 1958. The left frame of the stamp design shows a pair of golf clubs among other sporting paraphernalia. A French stamp of 1962 depicting the Paris Beach at Dunkirk shows a bag of golf clubs as part of the design (2). This completes the golf-related stamps; others are all "pure" golf.

The first pure golf stamp is a diamond-shaped 1962 issue of Cape Verde, part of a long series of stamps depicting various sports (3). An unusual golf stamp is the Nicaraguan air mail of 1963 depicting a tap-in (4). Monserrat has twice issued golf stamps, once for the 1967 International Tourist Year

(5), and again as part of a tourist issue of 1970.

The most spectacular golf stamp is a 1968 tourist stamp of the Bahamas. Its large, bold design is very attractive (6). Another unusual golf stamp is a 1969 triangle of Cook Island (7).

In 1971, two countries issued golf stamps: One was included in the series issued by French Polynesia for the Fourth South Pacific Games (8), and an entire set of four stamps devoted to the game was issued by Bermuda. This was the first time that the game of golf was actually an individual stamp issue, an honor usually reserved for top national and spectator sports and long overdue for golf. The four golf courses shown on the stamps are the Ocean View Golf Course (9); the Port Royal (10); Castle Harbour (11); and the Belmont (12). In 1974, Morocco issued a golf stamp to commemorate the Grand Prix International of Golf in Morocco and the "Hassan II" trophy.

The last items in this gallery of postal miniatures are the "Lunar golf" stamps. The one shown here is from Ras Al Khaima, one out of their 1971 set issued to honor the flight of Apollo XIV. It depicts Captain Alan B. Shepard, Jr., striking his smuggled golf ball (13). Another stamp with this design was issued in 1973 by Mali.

21. Graphic Arts Industry

At least fifty countries have recognized the importance of the graphic arts industry by issuing stamps depicting its early and important personalities, various printing presses, first products of their local printing industries, and important landmarks in the development of the industry.

American stamps issued for the graphic arts industry include several issues for the newspaper industry, particularly the 1958 Freedom of the Press Issue, which depicts an early press. One of the best illustrations of an early press to be found on any stamp appears on the United States stamp issued in 1939 to commemorate the three hundredth anniversary of printing in Colonial America. The stamp shows the first printing press brought to America in 1639 by an Englishman, Stephan Daye, who opened a printing shop at Cambridge, Massachusetts. The drawing for the stamp was made from the original press now housed in the Harvard University Museum.

In 1952, the five hundredth anniversary of the printing of the first book, the Holy Bible, from movable type, by Johann Gutenberg, was commemorated with a 3-cent stamp depicting the great printer and his assistant showing a proof of the Bible to the Elector of Mainz. Several other countries have issued stamps to honor Gutenberg as the inventor of movable type. Though the Chinese claim this invention as their own, no stamps of China were ever issued to back it up. Likewise, no Dutch stamp was ever issued for the other contender to the title, Laurence Coster of Haarlem. Germany has issued several stamps to honor Gutenberg; the one shown here was issued at the same time as was the American stamp.

Two other great German printers were honored with stamps. Ottmar Mergenthaler, the inventor (in 1886) of the Linotype, a hot metal linecasting machine, had a stamp issued in his honor in 1954, and the invention of the lithographic printing process (in 1796), by Alois Senefelder, was commemorated in 1972 by a stamp with a superb rendition of Senefelder's press.

Various countries have issued stamps honoring their first printers and/or the first works printed in that country. Bulgaria issued a "double" in 1940: One stamp shows the first Bulgarian printer, N. Karastayanov; the other honors Gutenberg. The first Russian printer, Ivan Fedorov, has been honored twice: in 1934 on the three hundred and fiftieth anniversary of his death, and in 1964 on the four-hundredth anniversary of book printing in Russia. The 1964 stamps show his statue in Moscow and a sixteenth century printer inking a form. The 1957 stamp of Cuba shown here reproduces the first publication printed in Cuba, an official price list of medicines.

The biggest stampic honor for graphic arts are two sets of three stamps each issued by Mexico in 1939 for the four hundredth anniversary of printing in Mexico (and in the Western Hemisphere). The stamps show the first engraving made in Mexico in 1544; the first work of legislation printed in America, 1563; reproduction of the oldest preserved Mexican printing; the first printing shop in the New World, Bell's Building in Mexico City, established in 1559; Friar Juan D. Zumarraga, who brought the first press from Seville to Mexico; and Viceroy Antonio D. Mendoza, who authorized the setting up of the first press in Mexico.

Ancient printers are on several stamps. A seventeenth-century priest-printer peeling off a printed sheet from the flat bed of a press is shown on the 1942 Finland commemorative of the three hundredth anniversary of the printing of the first Bible in the Finnish language (in 1642). A typesetter of a century ago appears on the 1963 Israeli commemorative marking the one hundredth anniversary of the Hebrew press in the Holy Land. The stamp was printed in sheets of sixteen; the background of the sheet shows a page of the first issue of the "Halbanon" newspaper, giving each stamp a different background.

Reproductions of newspaper pages are often used as a design for stamps issued to commemorate press anniversaries. The Argentine stamp shown here was issued in 1969 to commemorate the centenary of the newspaper La Prensa. The small stamp of Finland was issued in 1971 to honor the bicentenary of the Finnish press.

Government printing works appear on stamps of quite a few countries, though they usually reproduce various state security printing works engaged in the production of currency, stamps, and revenue paper. Some of these stamps also show printing presses; other stamps show just presses. The seventy-fifth anniversary of the Romanian State Printing Works commemorative of 1948 shows the printing plant and a press. An old printing press forms the design of the Austrian stamp issued in 1964 to publicize the Sixth Congress of the International Graphic Federation in Vienna.

A printing stamp was included in the 11 stamp set issued in 1948 by Hungary to commemorate the centenary of their war for independence. The stamp depicts an 1848 printing machine of the Albion type, still to be found in active service in some print rooms today—for pulling proofs.

The collector can find various other printing designs by browsing through catalogs. A colorful stamp of Switzerland, showing an inking unit, was issued in 1957 for the International Exhibition for Graphic Art at Lausanne. There are even stamps showing historicals—good collateral material for the collection. The oldest surviving writing, the cuneiform, is shown on a stamp of Austria issued in 1965. It portrays a stone table taken from an Assyrian palace. A clay tablet with the first alphabet is shown on a 1956 stamp of Syria. There are many others.

22. Guns

For the firearms enthusiast, the growing gallery of stamps depicting guns can be an interesting and challenging collection subject. The subject is still waiting for some devotee to make a count of all the stamps which show guns, but it's probable that all countries have issued them at one time or another.

In fact, there are so many stamps available with firearms in their designs that most collectors narrow the subject down to stamps which either depict the weapon as the principal part of their design, or to those which have been issued for some specific firearms-connected reason in which they are interested. In the first category fall the stamps that have been issued to show just weapons or which show the weapons clearly in the central part of the design. Sporting events and hunting fall into the second category.

Military stamps are a matter of individual taste. Their number is immense and unless one sets for himself a set of rules on their inclusion in the collection, it would be an almost impossible task to gather them all. Those military issues that show only the weapons or those which show armed men with the weapons prominent are suitable for inclusion in the first category above. There are not so many of them as to make it a chore to get them together.

Probably the most popular firearms stamps are those issued for sporting events. Not too many of them exist but the design is becoming very popular due to great interest in unusual Olympic designs, particularly the design of the rifleman on skis— the Biathlon.

The world's first stamp actually to honor a sport shooting event was issued by Sweden, in 1943, to commemorate the fiftieth anniversary of the Voluntary Shooting Association. The design, however, shows no guns—it's the emblem of the Rifle Federation. Such designs as emblems and trophies exist on some stamps and should be included in a collection of sport-shooting stamps. The first sport-shooting stamp actually to depict a firearm is the 1944 German issue for the Seventh National Shooting Matches at Innsbruck.

Many shooting events have been honored with stamps. One of the best sets in the genre comes from Romania, where it was issued in 1965 to commemorate the European Shooting Championships at Bucharest. The 20b value shows competition in small-bore rifle, kneeling; the 40b is rifle, prone; the 55b illustrates rapid-fire pistol; the 1.60L

shows small-bore rifle, standing; and the 2L stamp shows marksmen in various shooting postions. Other sport-shooting issues include one from the People's Republic of China. It was issued in 1959 for the First National Sport Meeting, Peking. A one-of-a-kind design showing a rifle and a target on a triangular stamp was issued in 1962 by UAR (Egypt). It commemorates the thirty-eighth World Shooting Championships.

Olympic shooting events account for most of the sport-shooting stamps. Shooting has been an Olympic event since the first Modern Olympiad was held in 1896, but the first stamp in honor of Olympic shooting was not issued until 1948. This is a stamp of Peru which shows a rifleman and celebrates the Peruvian gold medal in the pistol and the sixth place in the free-rifle competition at the fourteenth Olympiad in London.

Olympic shooting stamps are varied and colorful. Shown here are the 1964 Russian stamp issued for the Ninth Winter Olympic Games; a 1964 Hungarian issue for that year's Winter Olympics; and the stamps of Poland, Romania, and Andorra, issued for the Munich Olympics. The last stamp in this gallery was issued by the Dominican Republic and it's from the world's first set of stamps to identify Olympic winners by name. It shows Gerald Ouelette, the Canadian medalist in the small bore rifle in the 1956 Olympiad.

In the category of weapons on stamps, there are several "pure" designs—that is, just the firearm, or mainly the firearm. The "purest" of those is the Belgian stamp of 1967 issued to publicize the Fire Arms Museum in Liège. It shows a pistol by Leonhard Cleuter. An excellent set of gun stamps was issued in 1969 by Czechoslovakia. The six stamps show antique firearms: Cheb pistol,

circa 1580; Italian pistol with Dutch decorations, circa 1600; wheel lock rifle from Matej Kubik workshop, circa 1720; flintlock pistol from Devieux workshop at Liège, circa 1760; dueling pistols from Lebeda workshop in Prague, circa 1835; and American Derringer pistols, circa 1865.

The Derringers on the Czech set are not the only well-displayed American weapons on stamps. An excellent rendition of a Pennsylvania rifle appears on our 1968 stamp for Daniel Boone, one of the American Folklore Issues. Another A.F.I. stamp, the 1967 Davy Crockett stamp also shows a rifle of the period. There is also a rifle on the 1953 National Guard Issues and stacked rifles at Appomattox, 1965, are on one of the stamps issued for the Civil War Centennial. There are others.

Military weapons are on many stamps. Among the best are those issued by St. Helena. One of them shows a Baker rifle and a light sword bayonet, circa 1823; another depicts an English military pistol, circa 1800. A series of Mozambique showing various military units with their weapons makes an interesting showing of rifles. Those interested in stamps showing different military men with their weapons will find many such designs. They are usually listed in catalogs under "military uniforms." Often, some research and study will make it possible to identify the weapon. It's not easy.

Most military designs are also rather conventional with just about every type of a rifle pictured; the more recent designs include automatic weapons. Hunting weapons are fairly plentiful on stamps and there is a great variety of designs to pick from, though most of them are fairly conventional.

23. Horses and Horse Racing

With the issuance of a horse racing stamp to commemorate the one hundredth running of the Kentucky Derby, on May 5, 1974, the United States joined a club of at least 30 countries which have issued stamps in honor of horse racing.

From 1936 until the end of World War II, Germany was the only country issuing racing stamps. Austria joined her in 1946, but the design didn't really become popular until the 1960s. The early issues included a stamp for the Japanese Derby, in 1948, which also marked the twenty-fifth anniversary of the enforcement of Japan's horse racing laws, and a stamp of Brazil, the same year, for the centenary of the Jockey Club of Brazil. It was also the time of the Russian entry. Russia is a relative newcomer to this sport, but it is rapidly catching up and has issued stamps publicizing both its native breeds of horses. (Curiously enough, England, the home of modern horse racing, has never issued a racing stamp.) The Russian entry came in 1956, and commemorated the International Equestrian Events held in Moscow, in September of 1955.

Steeplechasing also joined the gallery dur-ing the 1950s. It first appeared on a stamp of Czechoslovakia, issued in 1956 to publicize the Pardubice Steeplechase. Not too many of these stamps have been issued, or, at least, not too many which can be definitely placed as racing stamps. Actually, the design is very popular and at least twice as many stamps with that design have been issued than racing designs, but most of these stamps depict horsemanship or cross-country racing and can't be properly included among true racing stamps.

Hungary is a prolific issuer of racing stamps and has issued several long, colorful sets of stamps depicting various scenes at the track. Other racing stamps have come from Afghanistan, East Germany, Poland, Mongolia, Bulgaria, Nicaragua, Saar, and Guatemala. The one hundredth running of the Melbourne Cup Race was commemorated in 1960 with an Australian stamp showing "Archer," the winner of the first running of the classic, in 1861.

The ancient sport of chariot racing, from which our modern harness racing developed, is a very old stamp design, dating back to 1896. The racing chariot, with a charioteer replacing the mythical goddess, was used several times on Greek stamps, and several other nations have used the design on stamps issued to honor the various Olympiads. Belgium used it in 1920, Liberia in 1956, Germany in 1960, and in 1965 it was used by Cyprus and Mauritania.

Modern harness racing—trotting—is American in origin, but the first trotting stamp was issued in 1956 by Russia, to commemorate the International Horse Races held in Moscow in September of 1955. At least seven other countries depicted trotters on their stamps, with Hungary in the lead with seven of them. *Cardigan Bay*, the great pacing champion from New Zealand—the first Standard-bred light-harness race horse to win a million dollars in stake money—was commemorated with a stamp of New Zealand in 1970. East Germany, Romania, Poland, and San Marino have also issued trotting stamps.

The latest use of racing stamps is to promote tourism. A large, spectacular "horse racing" stamp was included in the 1968 tourist propaganda set of the Bahamas, and in 1969, a series issued by Barbados depicted various scenes from the local track. In 1974, a similar set was issued by Togo. As racing is of great interest to tourists, more of these stamps can be expected from other countries in the near future.

Horse racing, though very interesting as a topical collection subject, is only a small part of a very large gallery of postal horses. Horses as such have appeared on many stamps, some issued in long sets showing various breeds. Other horses appear on farming stamps and the American Western horse has not been neglected. In fact, over 50 American stamps depict horses somewhere in their designs.

Various "horse" subjects can be built into a collection. The art of dressage can be almost completely depicted with postage stamps. Horses in mythology and horses in history are plentiful and the various styles of hunting on horses around the globe are shown on stamps of many nations. Fox hunts, boar hunts—even a lion hunt—you name it, it's on a stamp somewhere.

A great many equestrian statues are shown on stamps and the various horse-drawn wagons and mail coaches shown on stamps can form an interesting history of those conveyances.

The history of cavalry is also paraded for us on stamps: battles ancient and modern; armor and weapons of the riders; the different types of saddles and stirrups—they're all on stamps.

Other subjects include horses in literature, circus horses, medieval jousting, modern polo (and also some other locally played sports of various nations), and even toy horses.

24. Ice Skating

The world's leader in skating stamps is Russia, who entered the "skating" stamps club early in 1935, and has since issued them on at least seventeen different occasions. Ice skating is exceedingly popular in Eastern Europe and the postage stamp issues of those countries reflect the popularity of the sport and its recognition by the authorities. Hungary, Czechoslovakia, Romania, Poland, and Bulgaria have all issued stamps for numerous skating events. These countries between them have issued skating stamps on at least thirty-five different occasions. Nor have these been just single stamps. On the contrary, entire sets have been issued depicting men and women skaters in various events and different positions. Figure skaters and skating dancers have appeared on numerous issues of these countries.

Stamps issued for the Winter Olympic Games are now being issued around the globe in ever-increasing numbers, and many of these sets include stamps for the skating events. This has added to the skating stamps club countries where ice skating is virtually unknown, such as the various Arabian and African states. Still, the inclusion of skating stamps in the Olympic issues of those countries shows the great demand for them; otherwise they would not be included, since most of those stamps are sold to collectors and never see any postal service in their countries of issue.

The first Olympic skating stamp was issued by Germany for the IV Winter Games at Berlin, 1936. The V Games, in 1948, were not commemorated with a skating stamp, but in 1952, a skating stamp was issued by Norway for the VI Games at Oslo, and since then the skating stamp design has formed part of all designs for stamps issued for the Olympics. A number of skating stamps was issued for the XI Games at Sapporo.

World Figure Skating Championships have been depicted on stamps of a number of nations, including Canada, which issued one for the Championships held in 1972 at Calgary. Other skating stamps have been issued for various winter sport championships which include skating events. Many of the East European and Russian stamps have been issued for Spartacist Games, which are popular physical fitness events in that part of the world. Ice dancing competitions have also appeared on stamps, notably on those of Hungary, which has issued a number of them.

1. World's first skating stamp, issued by Hungary, in 1925.
2. Romanian stamp of pond skaters.
3. A Russian skating stamp: speed skating at Luzhniki Stadium, Moscow. Issued for the International Winter Sports Championships, Moscow, 1962.
4. Czechoslovakian stamp for the 1961 World Figure Skating Championships, Prague.
5. 1971 issue of Andorra for the World Figure Skating Championships held that year at Lyons, France.
6. Romanian stamp issued for the 1964 Winter Olympics.
7. The 1968 Grenoble Games commemorated with a stamp of the Trucial States sheikdom of Ras Al Khaima.
8. Stamp of San Marino issued to publicize the VII Winter Olympic Games at Cortina d'Ampezzo, 1956.
9. A Bulgarian skating stamp.
10. A skating stamp of Romania, issued for the Ninth World University Winter Games of 1951.
11. Stamp from a one-of-a-kind set of skating stamps from Hungary. This unusual series was issued in 1963 to commemorate the European Figure Skating and Ice Dancing Championships, Budapest.
12. Dominican stamp showing an American medalist of the 1956 Olympics at Cortina d'Ampezzo.
13. The 1972 Canadian issue for the World Championships.

25. Insects

For the insect enthusiast, the growing gallery of insect stamps can be an interesting and challenging subject and a "natural" combination: Those who enjoy live insects will find their paper counterparts no less interesting, and the serious entomologist will find all his knowledge necessary to build a blue-ribbon collection.

The postal gallery of insects is large, and growing larger every year. A count taken a few years ago showed that some 80 countries have issued insect stamps showing about 400 different species belonging to 57 families grouped in 7 orders. Just during one recent year, 12 countries issued 29 "insect" stamps.

The insect most often shown on postage stamps is the deadly, malaria-bearing mosquito of the genus *Anopheles*. Various species of this mosquito have been shown on stamps of some thirty nations, including the United Nations, as part of their anti-malarial campaigns. Its cousin, the yellow fever-bearing *Aëdes aegypti* has appeared on a stamp of Panama. Another killer in this order of Diptera is the little-known *Glossina morsitans*—the tsetse fly—a carrier of sleeping sickness. It is shown on the stamps of Cameroons, where the dreaded disease is still prevalent.

Another insect has recently become the object of a wide-spread campaign of extermination. It is the locust—once considered a tasty dish, but known as a plague insect since the beginning of recorded history. A member of the family of Acridiidae (short-horned grasshoppers), this destroyer of vegetation exists in several genera peculiar to different parts of the world. A dozen countries have issued stamps commemorating the "war on locusts."

Insects beneficial to mankind have been shown on stamps of many nations. The honey-bee—*Apis melliffica*—holds first place, with at least 10 countries issuing stamps in its honor. The silkworm moth, *Bombyx mori*, has been shown on stamps of several countries, but, curiously enough, neither China, where silk originated, nor Japan, which produces the finest silks, have issued stamps commemorating the spinner.

Not all insects appear on stamps with an entomological motif. The bee, for example, is often shown on stamps issued to publicize savings campaigns and on stamps issued to commemorate anniversaries of savings banks. (The ant is also sometimes used for savings designs.) The honeycomb design is also known on stamps with no connection with the bee or savings. It is sometimes used on stamps that display a range of national products or industries, with a symbolic design of each neatly depicted in each "window" of the honeycomb. Stamps of this nature lend themselves to the building of unusual collections, and even though their numbers are small, imaginative collectors have built prize-winning collections with just those specialized materials. (In addition to actual postage stamps, there are other philatelic materials available, such as postal stationery, cancellations, etc., and these add to the limited number of special-motif stamps.)

Perhaps the most famous of all insects is the scarabaeus, worshipped by ancient Egyptians as symbolic of resurrection and immortality. Also known as the scarab beetle, *Scarabaeus sacer*, it is a large black, or nearly black, dung beetle. Modern-day Egypt has gotten over her superstitions and has omitted the beetle from its stampic honors, but it does appear on a stamp of France.

Of the better-known insects, the ant appears on the stamps of East Germany and Poland. It is the great wood-ant, *Formica rufa*. Termites have not made it on stamps, but their nests have been pictured on stamps of several African nations. The various species of the genus *Bombus*, the bumble bee, are shown on stamps of Finland, Poland, and Switzerland. The beneficial, seven-spotted ladybird appears on stamps of a couple of countries and so does the praying mantis.

The moth and the butterfly appear on the stamps of almost all countries that have issued insect stamps. Some countries have issued stamps showing only those beautiful insects and no others. The swallowtails are probably the butterflies most often pictured. Dozens of species of this butterfly appear on stamps of many countries. The swallowtail itself, *Papilio machaon*, and its relative, the apollo butterfly, *Parnassius apollo*, vie for the honor of being most often depicted on a stamp. Other butterflies include the various cabbage butterflies, blues and coppers, and the many genera and species of the family Hymphalidae.

The family of the giant silkworm moth is well represented and includes the atlas moth, *Attacus atlas*, which appears on stamps of several Asian countries. The atlas moth is sometimes named as the biggest moth in the world, but in New Guinea and Australia lives the hercules moth, whose wings are less than ten inches across, but are so broad and ample that they reach a total surface area of nearly 100 square inches, probably making it the largest of all moths.

26. Iron and Steel Industries

The steel industry has been honored on hundreds of stamps issued by more than a score of nations. A smaller number of stamps honor the iron industry, though, naturally, many stamps are appropriate to both industries. There are two ways to collect this topic. One is to collect only those stamps which relate directly to the process of manufacture of the metal; another is to add to the collection stamps which show the uses of the metal in ships, locomotives, bridges, etc. In this chapter we will discuss only the stamps suitable for the first type of collection.

The United States has issued only one "steel" stamp—in 1957, for the centenary of the steel industry in America. (The date was taken from the 1857 patent by William "Pig Iron" Kelly, who patented a process of transforming pig iron directly into steel by using a current of air blown through it in a converter.)

Though the United States issued only one steel stamp, and none for the iron industry, the American iron industry *has* been honored on stamps ... of Bhutan, a tiny kingdom in the eastern Himalayas. The Bhutan Post Office has been very innovative in

issuing different kinds of stamps, many of them made from different materials than used for conventional stamp issues. In 1969, Bhutan scored one of its many postal "firsts" by issuing a set of stamps printed on steel foil.

Three of these stamps were issued with iron industry motifs. The Saugus, Massachusetts Ironworks, forms the design of the 15 ch. stamp. Founded in 1643, this ironworks is considered the birthplace of the American iron (and steel) industry. The 45 ch. stamp of the set depicts old beehive coke ovens, and the 2 ch. value portrays an ancient Assyrian furnace. Other stamps of this set depict a Bessemer converter, rolling mill, and a modern steel plant.

Blast furnaces, rolling mills, and molten steel being poured are the favorite designs of steel stamps. Others show the plants and steel mill workers. A good variety of designs shows many types of equipment and various mill operations, though the descriptions listed in stamp catalogs are not always correct. One can find a strip mill described as pipeworks or an electric arc steelmaking furnace labeled as a blast furnace.

Many nations have issued dozens of steel

stamps. Russia, for example, has issued stamps depicting various mills, equipment, and workers. The People's Republic of China has issued a number of steel industry stamps and so has Czechoslovakia. Tiny Luxembourg, which produces over one per cent of world's total steel production, has issued many stamps with steel themes including one (in 1960) showing a map of those countries holding membership in the European Coal and Steel Community. Other Luxembourg stamps have shown a steel beam, a six-link chain and a miner's lamp, a Bessemer converter and a blast furnace, and a panoramic view of steel mills.

Openings of steel mills are good occasions for issuance of special stamps. Perhaps the most colorful of these was issued by the Philippines, in 1970, for the opening of their first steel mill, the Iligan Integrated Steel Mills on Ligan Bay in Northern Mindanao. Another colorful design was used by Brazil, for their 1969 stamp, issued to commemorate the twenty-fifth anniversary of the Acesita Steel Works. Yet another colorful design is the 1957 Japanese steel industry centenary stamp showing modern steel plant alongside Japan's first blast furnace. One of the most graphic of all steel stamps is a small stamp issued by Japan in 1948, a 100 yen value showing a worker tending a fiery blast furnace.

Though the stamps relating directly to the iron industry are relatively few, they are interesting. The largest number of them have been issued by Russia. The best of these are two issued in 1929 as propaganda for greater industrial production. One stamp shows an iron furnace, with inscription reading "MORE METAL/MORE MACHINES!," while the other pictures a blast furnace and a chart of anticipated iron production. A later iron stamp, issued in 1946, commemorating the production of 50 million tons of cast iron, shows that the 1929 expectations were easily met.

Various countries have issued stamps showing the shaping of the hot metal. Some show the modern way, such as by use of a drop hammer, but most show the way it used to be done—by hand. In fact, the blacksmith is on enough stamps to form a small collection by himself.

Mining iron ore has been depicted on stamps, with the two best designs coming from Mauritania. One, issued in 1963, shows the Miferma open-pit mine at Zouerate; the other, issued in 1971, is actually a "double"— two stamps printed se-tenant (side-by-side) to form one large design. This double shows an iron ore freight train of Miferma Mines.

A1   A2   A3   A4   A5

B

C

D

E1

E2

F

G1

G2   G3   G4

27. Judaica

Philatelic Judaica is a topical specialty which embraces every stamp which by virtue of its subject matter is of Jewish interest. It's a very large subject but it can be easily broken down into manageable categories which can be built into interesting and educational collections.

Any stamp with the portrait of a Jew on it provides an opportunity to learn Jewish history and the contribution of Jews to civilization. An album of stamps of Jewish personalities annotated with brief biographies and contributions of the individuals would be an excellent Judaica collection.

Among the many Jewish personalities on stamps are Samuel Gompers, Albert Einstein, and Joseph Pulitzer, all on the stamps of the United States; there is Paul Ehrlich on a stamp of Germany and Leo Frankel on an issue of Hungary; Russian stamps portray Jacob M. Sverdlov and Anton Rubinstein; while Cuba has issued a stamp relating to

A. Jewish personalities: 1. Eric von Stroheim; 2. Sarah Bernhardt; 3. Karl Marx; 4. Samuel Gompers; 5. Albert Einstein.
B. The only Jew on an Arab stamp — Dr. Philip Blaiberg! The stamp was issued to show the world's first heart transplant and, unwittingly, portrayed a Jew — South African dentist, Dr. Philip Blaiberg (on the left on the stamp), who was the recipient of the transplant.
C. A stamp of the State of Israel depicting the Knesset Building.
D. Stamp of East Germany issued on the twenty-fifth anniversary of the *Kristallnacht* (Crystal Night) — the "Night of the Broken Glass" — an anti-Jewish outrage committed by the Nazis in 1938.
E. Stamps issued by Arab nations as anti-Israel propaganda: 1. Stamp of Kuwait issued to honor Palestinian commandos; 2. Egyptian stamp showing a dagger stuck into Israel.
F. A stamp of Czechoslovakia showing the tomb of David ben Solomon Gans, chronicler of Jewish historiography in the Bohemian countries.
G. Stamps commemorating the catastrophe of World War II: 1 and 2. Polish commemoratives of the death camp at Majdanek. 3. Polish commemorative of the death camp at Oswiecim. 4. Korean stamp of 1960 showing a Jewish grave, issued to commemorate the fifteenth anniversary of the United Nations.

the chess master, Emanuel Lasker. Jewish Nobel Prize winners on stamps include Michelson, Lippman, Niels Bohr, Bergson, and Adolf von Baeyer. Otto Loewi, Sarah Bernhardt, Max Reinhardt, Waldemar Hafkine, and Albert Ballin are just some of the hundred-plus Jews on stamps.

The State of Israel is, of course, the simplest and most obvious answer to a Judaica collection, and a good collection should include as complete a set of these stamps as one's pocketbook will permit. In addition to stamps, Israel postal services have always issued many interesting cancellations and slogans, and a collection of cancellations used for the opening of post offices can be used to illustrate the geography of the State of Israel. Along these lines, Zionist history can be illustrated with a collection of cancellations and slogans of the various Zionist Congresses and with stamps portraying leaders of Zionism.

The catastrophe of World War II can be amply illustrated with a Judaica collection. A number of stamps have been issued in memory of the victims of the Nazis, including some very good issues of Poland, East Germany, Czechoslovakia, France, and Russia. Other countries which have issued stamps suitable for this category are Austria, Belgium, Denmark, Dominican Republic, Britain (Jersey and Guernsey), Greece, Hungary, Italy, Jugoslavia, Korea. The Netherlands, Norway, and Somalia. In addition, many superb collections have been built from covers and post cards used in the ghettos and in the concentration camps.

Another category can deal with the stamps of the Arab nations issued as anti-Israel propaganda or in support of the Palestinian guerilla cause. There are a number of such stamps, issued by almost all Arab countries, many of them showing a dagger stuck into the map of Israel or some similar fighting motif. A good stamp here is one which was issued by Egypt in 1948. King Farouk was so confident of his ability to overrun the fledgling state that he ordered a stamp depicting Egyptian troops triumphantly marching into Israel. When the facts proved otherwise, the stamp was hurriedly withdrawn, but is still available to a collector of Judaica.

A good and extensive category is that of the Old Testament or Jewish religious references, quotations, symbols, personalities, etc. There are hundreds of stamps issued around the globe which can be fitted into such a collection. There are many stamps depicting various Biblical scenes and personalities. For example, the Vatican has a portrait of Elijah on a stamp and Saar has used Moses as a stamp subject. Adam and Eve, Bathsheba, King David, Prophet Joel, Balthazar, Moses' spy Caleb, and Samson and Delilah are just some of these personalities depicted on stamps. Abraham's Sacrifice, Jacob's Ladder, Mount Ararat, and the Judgment of Solomon are all on stamps, as are the Tables of the Law, David slaying Goliath, and Moses striking the rock. The Star of David, the dove, and the olive branch are frequent motifs.

Another category can be formed of non-Jewish personalities who aided and befriended Jews and the cause of Jewish freedom and played an important role in Jewish history. Here can be included such persons as Victor Hugo, Dante, Thomas Masaryk, Rembrandt, and many others. The portraits of all these men appear on stamps.

Other voluminous categories are works of art, literature, music, film, and architecture of or by Jews; scientific and international achievements in which Jews played a major role; and streets, squares, buildings, etc., named for Jews or used for Jewish purposes.

28. Law and the Legal Profession

"Lawyer" postage stamps fall into four categories: (1) those commemorating great legal events; (2) those depicting famous lawyers; (3) those picturing courthouses and legal structures; and (4) those containing legal symbols.

The United States entry in the first category is the 1953 commemorative of the seventy-fifth anniversary of the founding of the American Bar Association. A large variety of legal events has been commemorated on stamps of almost all nations. The signing of the Magna Carta, though not honored by British postal authorities, has been depicted abroad. The stamp shown here was issued by the United States in 1965 for the seven hundred and fiftieth anniversary of that event.

Other legal events commemorated with postal issues include the First National Judicial Congress in Brazil, in 1936, and the one hundredth anniversary of the Institute of Brazilian Lawyers, in 1943. Brazil possibly leads in this category. It has also issued stamps for the centenary of the founding of law courses in that country, for women's suffrage, and for the second Inter-American Conference of Lawyers. Latin American nations in general are prolific issuers of "lawyer" stamps. (Most of the stamps issued with legal motifs, of course, also contain legal symbols, thus combining that category with the others.)

Recent issues in the events gallery include a large spectacular from the Philippines, issued in 1971 for the sixtieth anniversary of the University of the Philippines Law College. The design, in striking colors, depicts an Allegory of Law. Another recent addition is the 1972 stamp of Korea for the Fifth Asian Judicial Conference in Seoul. Nineteen seventy-two also saw a Mexican commemorative for the fiftieth anniversary of the Mexican Bar Association. The design is the head of the Emperor Justinian. Two other stamps with that motif form the Lebanon issue of 1968, issued to honor Beirut as the site of one of the greatest law schools in antiquity, and to honor Emperor Justinian, who compiled and preserved the Roman law.

Many stamps picture lawyers. Cuba has issued several stamps showing her lawyers; the one shown here pictures Jose A.

Gonzalez Lanusa and forms part of a set of four different lawyer stamps. American poet Edgar Lee Masters was honored with a special stamp in 1970. He was also a lawyer (lawyers on stamps are not always obvious). A stamp of Mauritius, part of a set issued to commemorate the centenary of the birth of Mohandas K. Gandhi, shows him as a young law student in London. A stamp showing a symbolic lawyer was issued in 1968 by Gabon for the International Human Rights Year.

Sir Francis Bacon is pictured on a stamp of Newfoundland, Ireland's Daniel "The Liberator" O'Connell is on stamps of Eire, and Sir Charles Coghlan, first premier of Southern Rhodesia, appeared on a stamp of that nation in 1940. Sir John A. Macdonald, first Prime Minister of the Dominion of Canada, and Canadian prime ministers Robert Baldwin and Sir Georges Etienne Cartier are on stamps of Canada. Baldwin was a former solicitor-general of Upper Canada, while Cartier was former attorney-general of the Dominion.

The category of courts and court houses is very large. The U.S. Supreme Court building is on stamps and so is the court house at Beira, Mozambique. Modern courthouses are on stamps of Panama, the Dominican Republic, and of many other countries. The five hundredth anniversary of the Berlin Court of Appeals was commemorated by a German issue of 1968, while the fiftieth anniversary of the Icelandic Supreme Court was commemorated in 1970, with a stamp showing the first meeting of the court. Just about every better-known courthouse is on stamps, and so are many lesser-known buildings, such as, for example, the court house at Belize, in British Honduras. The International Court, The Hague, is shown here on a stamp of Cameroun, issued in 1971 for its twenty-fifth anniversary.

Another group of stamps exists showing actual court scenes. Most of these are from the Communist nations and depict various martyrs to the Red Cause being tried. Probably most of those countries have issued such stamps. The one here, from Bulgaria, shows Dimitrov facing Goering, during the Reichstag trial. The world's best known court scene, that of *The Merchant of Venice*, is shown on a stamp of Senegal.

The category of legal symbols is mostly confined to the Scale of Justice, which appears on untold numbers of stamps. The ones here are from the United States and Iran. The first commemorates the Workmen's Compensation Law; the second was issued in 1969 to publicize the Fifteenth General Assembly of Women Lawyers in Teheran. The motif is also a favorite of United Nations stamps.

Various symbols of justice appear on a French stamp of 1957, issued for the one hundred and twenty-fifth anniversary of the French Cour des Comptes. Mr. Law himself, Hammurabi, is on a stamp of Iraq issued in 1964 to commemorate the fifteenth anniversary of the Universal Declaration of Human Rights.

29. Lions International

Lions International has been the object of many postal honors from around the globe, and the Lion interested in becoming a *Lion-topicalist*—as such collecting Lions are called by their fellow philatelists—will have no difficulty in forming an interesting collection.

Some 165 stamps and souvenir sheets have been issued by over 50 nations for Lions International. The largest number of these, close to one hundred, have been issued by almost 90 nations during the Golden Jubilee Year of 1967 in honor of the fiftieth anniversary of the organization. Forty-two Lion stamps existed prior to 1967, and several have been issued each year since.

The first Lion stamp was issued by Cuba, in 1940, to honor the International Convention held that year at Havana. Another early Lion issue (four stamps) came from the Philippines in 1950, on the occasion of the first convention of District 301, and two more stamps were issued in 1952 to commemorate the Third District Convention at Baguio City. Brazil is another multiple issue country, with the first Lion stamp issued there in 1965 in honor of the XIIth Convention of Multiple District L (Brazil) held that year in Rio de Janeiro.

Nicaragua issued two sets of six stamps, one for ordinary postage and one for air mail, and two souvenir sheets in 1958, for the XVIIth Convention of District D, Istmania. This is the largest single issue of Lion stamps anywhere. Another large set, six stamps, was issued by Rwanda for the sixtieth anniversary, and a four-stamp set was issued for the same occasion by Togo, but the country with the largest anniversary issue was Paraguay, which came in with 12 stamps— six ordinary and six air mail.

Other early Lion stamp issues include a set of three stamps issued by Cameroons in 1962 to honor the help of the Lions in combatting leprosy and World Day of Leprosy. The stamps were surcharged (carried an extra price) for the benefit of the activity fund of the Cameroons Lions. China (Taiwan) was also a Lion stamp country before the anniversary; it issued a stamp in 1962 to honor the forty-fifth anniversary of Lions International. Another early stamp (and a companion souvenir sheet) was issued in 1966 by Korea to honor the Fifth Orient and Southeast Asian Lions Convention held in Seoul.

In Europe, San Marino issued a set of six Lion stamps in 1960 to celebrate the founding of the Lions Club of San Marino, and Monaco celebrated the founding of their Lions Club (organized in 1961; charter presented in 1962) with a stamp issued in May of 1963.

Panama, which issued seven Lion stamps, is one of the favorites of Liontopicalists, the reason being various errors made in the production of the stamps.

More recent Lion issues have come from Laos, Senegal, Argentina, Korea, Mexico, and the Netherland Antilles. The largest post-anniversary issue is from Salvador, which issued four triangular stamps in 1973 on the occasion of the thirty-first District D Convention at San Salvador, held in May of 1972.

Of course, not only the events honored with the stamps are interesting, so are the many Lions depicted on the various stamps. Melvin Jones, Founder and Secretary General of Lions International, is portrayed on stamps of Nicaragua, San Marino, Monaco, and Paraguay. Other Lions on stamps include Teodoro A. Arias, of Ancon, Panama Canal Zone; and Edward G. Berry, Little Rock, Arkansas, both on stamps of Nicaragua. Finis E. Davis, elected president of Lions International in 1960, is on a stamp of San Marino, and so is Clarence L. Sturm, elected International President in 1959. (San Marino also made him a Commander of the Order of Saint Agatha.)

In addition to postage stamps, Liontopicalists have at their disposal a vast number of very colorful and interesting covers issued for conventions and special and Lionistic events. Particularly interesting are the covers issued for various "air" events. These go back to the dedication of Roswell, New Mexico, airport in 1929!

30. Masonry

For many years philatelic Masonry has been a very popular topic both with Masons who are stamp collectors, and with those who are not collectors but are interested in learning about famous Masons appearing on stamps. Thus, the Mason-collector always has a ready and interested audience when it's time to show his collection.

Through the efforts of Mason-collectors, two books and many articles have been written identifying Masons on stamps and listing their biographies. Other articles have listed Masonic symbols, Masonic Postal History, Masonic events, and many other related information on Masonry and philately.

Over 400 Masons have been identified on stamps, and the subject of personalities is large enough to lend itself to collecting them in sections according to one's personal preference. Some collect Masons by country, while others build specialized sections, such as presidents or foreign kings. Other sections can be built according to desire. For example, one might form a collection of Mason musicians, or Masons who were patriots and soldiers.

Since many Masons are shown on a number of stamps the possibility presents itself to show more than one stamp, perhaps illustrating various events in the life of the subject. For example, Britain's King George VI appears on a number of stamps of Britain and her Colonies. A selection of these could include the King in mufti and in his naval uniform, the King with his Queen, and the Royal Couple with their children, plus a few colonial stamps appropriate to the theme. The write-up, whenever possible, should include as much factual Masonic information as possible and the stamps should be pertinent to the write-up. In this case, King George VI was initiated in Naval Lodge No. 2612 of London, December, 1919. Thus, a stamp depicting him in a naval uniform is very pertinent.

An interesting collection can be formed of Masonic symbols, and a number of stamps can be found which are suitable to this theme. The Acacia can be found on stamps of Australia; The All-Seeing Eye can be shown with stamps of Egypt, the United States, and Argentina; and the Altar, Astronomy, and the Holy Bible can be found on many stamps. The Cedars of Lebanon are on stamps of that nation, and Cleopatra's Needle is on two stamps of Egypt. Broken columns are found on stamps of Albania, Austria, Cyprus, Honduras, and Italy. It takes some looking around—and some imagination—to come up with appropriate designs, but a diligent search can produce many stamps with Masonic symbols.

The Compass, for example, can be found on many stamps, and so can the Double Headed Eagle and the Rose. On the other hand, the Seven-Branched Candlestick is only on one stamp of Israel and the Pot of Incense on a single issue of Spain. Other Masonic symbols which can be located on stamps are the Letter G; the Hoodwink; Corn, Wine, and Oil; the Keystone; Mallet and Chisel; the Masonic Rod; the Square; the trowel; and many others.

Famous Masons on stamps:
1. José de San Martin.
2. Gen. Douglas MacArthur.
3. Sir Charles Kingsford-Smith.
4. Marquis de Lafayette.
5. Gen. Casimir Pulaski.
6. Samuel Gompers.
7. Benjamin Franklin.

Masonic symbols on stamps:
A. The Trowel on a stamp of Great Britain.
B. The All-Seeing Eye on stamp of Egypt.
C. Masonic Temple on a stamp of Honduras.
D. The Mace on a stamp of Canada.
E. The Bible on stamp of Finland.
F. Square and Compass on stamp of Germany.
G. This Canadian stamp shows 11 symbols which can be associated with the Masonic order: Gavel, Set Square, Sun, Moon, and Star, the Globe, Plumb, Alpha and Omega, Math signs, Man, Greek Temple, and Pencil.

31. Medicine

Physicians interested in collecting medical subjects that appear on stamps are in a very fortunate position. Not only will they have no difficulty filling volumes regarding their topic, but theirs is one of the best researched subjects in all stampdom. No matter what his specialty, the physician-collector not only has a wealth of postal material available at his disposal, but hundreds of articles, dozens of books, and up-to-date bulletins are available to help him build an interesting collection.

Medical philately embraces all the facets of the profession. Thousands of stamps, issued by almost all nations, portray physicians, medical scientists, medical events, hospitals, human anatomy, medical symbols, paramedical services, medical equipment and instruments, ambulances, medical laboratories, and natural sources of medicinal drugs. (Red Cross and nursing form separate collecting specialties.)

The largest section of medical philately comprises physicians. Hundreds of doctors appear on stamps, including many who distinguished themselves in fields other than medicine. There are ancient practitioners, surgeons and anatomists, ophthalmologists,

radiologists and physicists, neurologists and psychiatrists, medical missionaries and medical humanitarians, educators, geneticists, bacteriologists and epidemologists, and even fadists and healers. And there are those medical truants who distinguished themselves as explorers and colonizers, poets and writers, statesmen, patriots, and politicians.

In addition to stamps there is available an enormous amount of collateral material, such as special cancellations and cachets for medical events, postal slogans, postal stationery, and other similar material which makes a collection more complete and more interesting.

Medico-historical philately not only lends itself to building interesting stamp collections but it can be a strong intellectual stimulus, leading to the exploration in greater detail of the evolution of medicine, its colorful medical truants and scientists, and the progress of medicine.

Within the specialties of the profession individual collections can be built embracing large or small topics of individual interest. For example, for the radiologist, the field offers the possibility of forming an extensive collection depicting the complete history of the discipline starting with Democritus and ending with the latest in X-ray equipment. The hematologist will find a profusion of stamps depicting blood, and the cardiologist will find hearts of every shape including the picture of the physician who had two. (He was Baron Corvisart de Marets. He had his own heart, and another a gift of Napoleon Bonaparte, which he incorporated into his Coat of Arms when Napoleon named him a baron.)

Even an interest in a specific disease can be the basis for an interesting collection. Tuberculosis, cancer, leprosy, malaria, and poliomyelitis are just some of the sicknesses against which the postage stamp has been used as a weapon of awareness. Currently, the world-wide interest in drug abuse has stimulated many postal issues on this topic, and many stamps are being issued on the subject of mental health and the rehabilitation of the handicapped.

In fact, if one really likes to specialize in just one thing, there is nothing like a collection of stamps depicting Dr. Sun Yat-Sen. There exist about 2500 major and minor varieties of stamps showing the Chinese president who was also a physician. Such collections *have* been formed!

Other possibilities in the topic of medical collecting include medical mythology and symbols. A fertile field, it lends itself to research and study. Despite the fact that medical philately has been extensively studied, new discoveries are still made in this specialty.

The United States stamps offer many possibilities in medical philately. American medical philately goes back to 1869, when the United States issued a stamp reproducing Trumbull's "Signers of the Declaration of Independence." Among this group of the fathers of the United States were five physicians, three of whom can be identified on the stamp: J. Bartlett, B. Rush, and O. Wolcott. There are at least 50 other American stamps directly related to medicine, plus a large number of cancellations, cachets, and postal slogans.

32. Mining

Just about every country that has a mining industry has issued stamps depicting it.

Coal and salt, copper, bauxite and manganese; emeralds and diamonds; silver and iron ore; copper and nickel are just some of the mining operations shown in stamps. Just about every imaginable mining operation can be found on a stamp somewhere, from an old-timer panning for gold to a floating dredge operating on alluvial cassiterite deposits. Some of the stamps show in great detail many important mining operations, others are symbolic designs, and yet others show miners. Each year dozens of stamps are added to this gallery, as new mining operations are honored equally by the governments of the newly independent nations and by those where mining has been going on for hundreds of years.

Some countries have issued only a couple of stamps for their mining industry, others have issued as many as a hundred. Saar, for example, where mining is a way of life, has issued over one hundred mining stamps depicting in great detail the many aspects of the industry. Zambia, independent only since 1964, has already issued three mining stamps, two for the copper mining industry and one for coal.

Coal mining is by far the leading mining-stamps design; probably more stamps have been issued for coal mining than for all the rest of the industry together. Iron ore is probably the runner up, and this is reasonable, for these are basic industries common to many nations, particularly in Europe, where most of the coal stamps have been issued. Mining for gold and precious stones is a very popular design which can be found on the stamps of the nations with deposits of precious ores. The expanding use of various metals can be seen in the number of stamps being issued for the mining aspects of that industry. The aluminum industry, for example, has given birth recently to a number of stamps showing bauxite mining operations, including an interesting historical issue from Surinam. Tin and copper mining is also becoming a more common stamp design and, of course, uranium mining has also found a place in the gallery.

The great variety of designs of mining stamps is one of the most appealing reasons for collecting them. Almost a complete primer on mining can be illustrated with

stamps. Headframes alone could form a couple of pages in a mining stamps collection, and a section on how not to do it could be included as well, for a number of stamps exist showing artists' errors. There is a headframe with the leg in the wrong position, another with too many cables, and another yet with the wheel touching its side.

If mining railways are your fancy you will have no problem in depicting them in a small collection: At least 25 countries have issued 55 stamps showing mining railways. Another interesting subject is a collection of historicals, showing the progress in the industry. Many stamps have been issued showing ancient equipment, and all kinds of interesting historical subjects can be shown with mining stamps once you get "into" the subject. For example, a miner's lamp can serve to dress up a page of stamps. You'll find stamps showing ancient oil lamps, a carbide lamp with a reflector, the Davy lamp, and the electric storage battery lamps, first carried by hand, and later with the battery carried on a belt and the lamp attached to the miner's cap.

Other mining subjects are surface mining, symbolic allegories representing the mining industry, miners' tools, and, of course, there exists a wealth of collateral material such as special cancellations and cachets used on the first day of the stamps' issue or for special mining events, souvenir sheets, postal stationery with mining industry stamps impressed on it, and various other items the collector will become aware of once he enters the hobby.

33. Money

"Cash money"—coins and paper currency—is rapidly becoming a subject worthy of honoring on postage stamps. Prior to 1950 only 16 countries issued stamps depicting money in their designs, but during the past 20 years this number rose to over 60. There now exist over 500 stamps portraying money in their designs.

The United States has never issued a stamp showing money—the closest we came to it is with the symbolic coin shown on the 1950 commemorative of the seventy-fifth anniversary of the founding of the American Bankers Association. However, American money has been pictured on stamps of foreign countries.

A 1966 stamp of the Philippines shows a United States one peso silver coin of 1903-1912. At the time of the mintage, the Philippines was a U.S.-administered territory. A souvenir sheet issued by the Philippines the same year reproduces a complete 50 pesos 1916 United States note for use in the Philippines. A stamp showing national products is superimposed in the center of the bill. The two stamps were issued to commemorate the fiftieth anniversary of the Philippine National Bank. In 1968, the Trucial States sheikdom of Ras al Khaima issued two stamps showing the Kennedy half-dollar. This coin is also shown on a stamp of Nigeria.

Some banknotes have been pictured on stamps, but most of the money stamps show coins. Current and ancient coinage, silver and gold coins as well as non-precious metal coinage, all have been shown on stamps, but countries which have been issuing coins since the beginning of minted coinage—Greece, Crete, Bulgaria, Cyprus—have tended to portray mostly the ancient coins showing their history through the ages. Interestingly enough, China, where coins were first used, has never issued a stamp showing money. The same situation exists in Egypt, said by Herodotus to have originated the idea of minting coins as early as 1780-1580 B.C. Other chroniclers say coinage had its birth in Asia Minor with the Cappadocia civilization and others yet claim honors for the Cretan city of Knossos. The Ariadne, an ancient coin of Knossos, vintage about 500-400 B.C., is shown on a stamp of Crete issued in 1905. However, most historians favor giving credit for minting the first coins to the Lydians, during the reign of King Gyges (circa 700 B.C.). Turkey, the site of ancient Lydia, is another country without a coin stamp.

An interesting coin shown on a stamp is

the Menelik Dollar, which served as the design of a set of stamps of Ethiopia issued in 1894. Named after the Ethiopian ruler, Menelik II, the coin was struck in silver at the Paris mint, in an effort to replace the 150-year-old Maria Theresa thaler, a coin to this day accepted as a universal trade dollar.

Early Bermudian Hogge money from Sommer Island, probably the first coins struck in North America, are pictured on several Bermudan stamps of 1953. They were named "Hogge" because of a hog on the obverse of the coins. Coins were minted around 1616.

The first money stamp issued in the Western Hemisphere was issued by El Salvador in 1921. It shows a Confederation gold coin of 1823. Another early Latin stamp is the 1936 Brazilian commemorative issued for the first Numismatic Congress at Sao Paulo. It is of unusual design, in that it pictures a coinage press. In 1968, Chile also issued a stamp with a coinage press in its design to honor the two hundred and twenty-fifth anniversary of the founding of the State Mint.

Banknotes are shown on stamps of Norway, the Dominican Republic, Biafra, Greece, Uruguay, and Cuba, and an Italian stamp shows banknotes and a bank book. Coins and bank books can be seen on stamps of Cameroons and Upper Volta. An unusual design is one of a 1960 stamp of New Caledonia, showing a girl operating a check writer. It was issued to commemorate the centenary of the first postal money order.

In 1968, Venezuela issued a stamp to publicize the National Savings System. The stamp shows a piggy bank and a hand inserting a coin into it. A Korean stamp issued in 1966 to publicize systematic savings, shows a money bag and a honeycomb. A savings bank pass book is shown on Romanian stamps issued for the same reason in 1956.

Something "different" in money stamps is a Japanese stamp of 1964. It shows coin-like emblems, marked IMF, IBRD, IFC, and IDA. It was issued to commemorate the annual general meeting of International Monetary Fund, International Bank for Reconstruction and Development, International Financial Corporation, and International Development Association in Tokyo, September 7-11. Another unusual stamp was issued in 1971 by Malaysia to honor a banking anniversary. It shows no money, but is itself in the shape of a coin and has a double row of perforations which make it possible to separate the coin design from the normal stamp square. It exists in two values, one printed in silver, the other in gold color.

Money stamps have been issued to commemorate historical events and to honor rulers, ancient and modern, shown on coins; to commemorate various banking and banking-related anniversaries; to commemorate first coinages; to promote savings; and simply to produce interesting-looking stamps that will sell well to stamp collectors, particularly to the new breed called topical collectors. The world-wide spread of topical collecting is the reason for such unusual coin stamps as Tonga's odd-shaped stamps on foil, the Malaysian stamp mentioned above, the set of Bahama's crescent-shaped stamps, engraved on gold paper (to commemorate the first gold coinage in the Bahamas); the Kennedy half-dollars issued by foreign countries; and many others. Of the 500-plus money stamps in existence, over 100 have been issued by Greece and some 50 by Israel. The balance is divided among the other countries.

34. Music

The nations of the world have long been issuing postage stamps depicting their cultural heritage. In this large gallery of postal miniatures, the world of music holds first place. More than 3000 stamps with musical designs have been issued around the world. Some depict composers, authors, lyricists, and librettists; others display a full range of musicians— conductors, singers, pianists, violinists, etc.; while hundreds of designs form almost a complete gallery of musical instruments used around the globe since the dawn of history. Other stamp motifs are compositions— annotated or depicted— musical associations, opera houses, personalities, conservatories, scenes from operas, musical excerpts, etc.

This interesting and growing gallery of musical stamps can be a challenging subject. Music on stamps is among the ten most popular stamp topics in the world and many prize-winning collections at stamp shows are topical collections with music themes. Particularly in demand at these shows are collections showing the lives and works of great composers.

The wide variety of musical motifs offers a splendid opportunity to collect precisely what best strikes one's fancy. Even seeming-ly small subjects are fertile grounds for blue-ribbon displays. Take National Anthems. At least 45 countries have issued stamps related to that subject— more than enough for a large collection. The United States entries in this gallery are two stamps related to Francis Scott Key. One was issued in his honor in 1948, the other depicts his signature, and was issued in 1960.

Whatever motif is selected, a collection of musical stamps offers the builder many opportunities to learn about his "paper" music. For example, in 1961, Iran issued a stamp for the International Congress of Music at Teheran. The musician shown on the stamp is described in the stamp catalog as Safiaddin Amavi. Safiaddin turns out to be his first name, though it's properly Safi al-din, but Amavi turns out to be the catalog editor's fancy, for his real name is actually 'Abd al-Mu'min ibn Faquir al-Urmawi al-Baghdadi. He was a thirteenth-century Persian-Arabian musician, chief minstrel to the last 'Abbasid caliph al-Musta'sim. We'll skip his life's story (he fell on evil ways and died in debtor's prison) and only mention some of his musical achievements. These include the invention of two stringed instruments, the mughani and the nuza, and the authorship of

several musical treatises, including the Kitab al-adwar (Book of Musical Modes).

Those with more conventional tastes, and lesser desires to write Persian names in English alphabet, can concentrate on American postal music. The United States has issued over 40 stamps featuring musical instruments and musicians. Foreign countries have honored American musicians and personalities related to music, such as, for example, Benjamin Franklin, credited with being the first printer and publisher of music in America. Franklin played the harmonica, violin, harp, and guitar, and composed songs. He once gave a harmonica recital which was attended by George Washington.

Among our stamps depicting musical instruments is the 1964 American Music Issue to commemorate the fiftieth anniversary of the founding of the American Society of Composers, Authors, and Publishers. A lute and a horn are included in the design. Another "instruments" stamp is the 1969 issue to honor William Christopher Handy, depicting him with a clarinet. An angel blowing a straight horn is on the Christmas stamp issued in 1965. Bells in the belfry of the Carmel Mission are shown on the commemorative of the two hundredth anniversary of the settlement of California, issued in 1969, and a military drummer is on a stamp issued in 1929. There are others.

A number of professional musical performers have been honored on stamps. The first professional honored on United States stamps was John Philip Sousa. He appeared on a 1940 stamp, one in the series of Famous Americans. In the same series honors were extended to Victor Herbert and Edward Alexander MacDowell. The professional musician who was also a great statesman, Ignace Paderewski, was honored in 1960 with a stamp in the series of Champions of Liberty.

Black American musicians have been honored by several African nations. Louis Armstrong has appeared on stamps of Gabon and Upper Volta. Jimmy Smith was honored by Upper Volta in 1972, and Duke Ellington is on a stamp of Togo, one out of a set issued for the twentieth anniversary of UNESCO (United Nations Educational, Scientific and Cultural Organization). The Gabon set of stamps honoring black American musicians also included stamps in honor of Nat King Cole and Sidney Bechet.

35. New York City

More stamps, American *and foreign,* picture the City of New York than any other city in the world. In fact, it's quite possible that New York City has been depicted on more stamps than all the major cities in the world put together!

The City of New York— buildings, bridges, statues, and the pavilions in its World's Fairs — has been pictured on hundreds of stamps. Other "New York stamps" show the City's airports, details from paintings in its art galleries and museums, and paintings showing old New York. Of course, it is the United Nations complex which makes up the vast majority of stamps which show New York's buildings, but even before the United Nations buildings began to appear on stamps around the globe, New York's Statue of Liberty and its World's Fair buildings appeared on many American and foreign stamps.

New York City stamps can be divided into eight categories: views of Manhattan, bridges of New York, statues of New York, 1939 World's Fair, 1964 World's Fair, named buildings, United Nations, and miscellaneous.

The views of Manhattan category is sort of arbitrary because many of these stamps also show the U.N. buildings and/ or the Statue of Liberty. However, some 20 stamps show particularly good views of Manhattan and can be placed in this category. Included here are the stamps of Sharjah and Monaco shown on the photo page, the 15-cent U.S. air mail of 1947, stamps of Russia issued to honor O. Henry and William Foster, and the U.N. commemoratives of Mauritania, Haiti, Lebanon, and Guinea. Other nations whose stamps picture Manhattan are Israel, Antigua, San Marino, Colombia, Yemen, Switzerland, Greece (a night view), Samoa, and Congo. A spectacular view of the entire isle of Manhattan is on a 1969 stamp of Czechoslovakia.

Bridges of New York are the Verrazano-Narrows Bridge on stamps of the United States, Italy, and British Honduras, and the George Washington Bridge on a United States stamp of 1952, issued to commemorate the centenary of the founding of the American Society of Civil Engineers.

Statues of New York include the Atlas holding up the globe at Rockefeller Center, on stamps of Germany; the statue of Simon Bolivar on the edge of Central Park, on stamps of Venezuela; and a Jugoslavian stamp showing the "Peace" statue and several foreign renditions of the Sword-into-Plowshare statue at the United Nations. At least 25 stamps depict the Statue of Liberty in such detail as to place them in this category. Besides eight American stamps with this motif, there are stamps from Bulgaria, Nicaragua, Peru, Philippines, Panama, Uruguay, Korea, and China, to name just some of the nations which have depicted the Statue of Liberty on their stamps.

The 1939 World's Fair pavilions and its symbols of Trylon and Perisphere are on stamps of the United States, Russia, Nicaragua, France, Mexico, and the Dominican Republic, and these might not be all that can be found. In addition, 1939 World's Fair stamps, all in the same design, were issued by 24 different French colonies.

The 1964 World's Fair is shown by its pavilions or its Unisphere symbol on many more stamps than was the 1939 event. At least 15 different countries have issued such stamps, some of them quite spectacular in color and design. Particularly good designs have come from Jordan, Guinea, Togo, and Ireland. Some of the nations which have shown their pavilions on stamps are Indonesia, China, Venezuela, Korea, and Sudan.

The named buildings is an interesting category and it covers only stamps showing a single building or those where the building is predominant in the design. The Empire State Building is on stamps of Yemen, Ecuador, and in the background of the LaGuardia commemorative shown on the photo page. The Coliseum is on stamps of the U.S., Liberia, and Russia; Federal Hall is on an American stamp, and so is the Low Library at Columbia University; and the Main Post Office building is on a stamp of Monaco.

The United Nations buildings complex is on a large number of stamps, perhaps one hundred or more, some of them issued by the United Nations, others by member nations. Some of the best designs are on the stamps of the United Nations and the issues of Togo, Cameroons, and Guinea.

The miscellaneous category is the catch-all group for stamps that are not found in sufficient number to be classified in groups by themselves. Here we include historical views, two of which are shown on the photo page, the airports— Idlewild (later Kennedy International)— and stamps reproducing works of art located in New York City. There is also a U.S. air mail stamp depicting the five boroughs of New York.

A collection of New York on stamps can be extended to include those issued for special and first flights from and to New York (there are many of these) and those showing New Yorkers, native-born and otherwise, some well-known to New Yorkers, others renowned in their native lands.

36. Nursing

More than 800 stamps issued by more than 120 countries exist in honor of nurses and nursing. This is remarkable, in view of the fact that the first postage stamp was issued only 134 years ago and that modern nursing is only about 100 years old.

Some nursing stamps have been issued in honor of specific nurses, while others have been issued to honor the profession in general. At least 30 nursing personalities have been honored on stamps of about 50 nations. Florence Nightingale, "The Lady with the Lamp," leads the list of individual nurses honored by stamps; she has been honored by eight nations.

The only American professional nurse shown on a stamp is Clara Louise Maass, but she appears on a stamp of Cuba issued in 1951. She was a U.S. Army nurse who worked with General William Gorgas in combatting yellow fever in Cuba. She let herself be bitten by a mosquito and died a martyr to science.

Clara Barton, founder of the American Red Cross, and Louisa May Alcott have been pictured on our stamps. Miss Alcott worked as a nurse during the Civil War. American poet Walt Whitman also served as a hospital nurse during the Civil War. He is on the stamps of Bulgaria, Romania, and the United States.

Edith Louisa Cavell, a British nurse who worked in Belgium at the start of World War I, was shot by the Germans in 1915 for helping wounded Allied soldiers to escape. She was honored with a stamp of Costa Rica, on which she appears together with Florence Nightingale. She is also the object of a philatelic honor once-removed: A Canadian peak named after her, Mount Cavell in Alberta, is on a stamp of Canada.

Other nurses on stamps include Amalie Sieveking on a stamp of Germany. She founded the Woman's Organization for Nursing Sick and Poor in 1852, and was a volunteer nurse in Hamburg during a cholera epidemic. In 1967, Brazil honored Ana Justina Neri, an Army nurse during the War with Paraguay (1865-1870). The Ana Neri School of Nursing in Rio de Janeiro, founded in 1923, was the first nursing school in South America. Another German stamp honors the "Angel of Siberia," Elsa Brandstrom. She received the nickname for her work among German prisoners of war in Siberia during the typhus epidemic of 1919-1920.

There are also stamps in honor of St. Elizabeth of Hungary and St. Catherine of Siena; Sister Mary Aikenhead, founder of the Irish Sisters of Charity; Manuelita de La Cruz

of Colombia; Cathinka Guldberg, who founded the Deaconess Institute in Norway (first step toward modern nursing in Norway); and Victora Bru Sanchez of Cuba.

Pastor Theodore Fliedner was honored by a German stamp issued in 1952. He and his wife Frederike founded the Kaiserwerth Deaconess Institution in Germany, where Florence Nightingale took her early schooling.

The Continental vogue to have royalty appear in a nurse uniform started with a Romanian stamp of 1906 that pictures Queen Elizabeth. Continental royalty in nurse uniforms on stamps includes Queen Marie of Romania, Queen Victoria Eugenia of Spain, Princess Charlotte of Monaco, and Princess Josephine-Charlotte of Belgium.

Some stamps issued to honor nursing anniversaries are interesting. The 1957 stamp of Belgium issued to commemorate the fiftieth anniversary of Belgium's first school of nursing shows Queen Elizabeth in nurse uniform assisting a surgeon. The Queen was not a nurse, but a fully qualified medical doctor.

The 1961 American nursing stamp depicted a symbolic student nurse and was issued to mark the centenary of American schools of nursing. It caused some controversy as historians generally agree the founding date was 1873, not 1861. The student nurse did not turn out to be a nurse, but a professional model, Susan Bernstein.

The Canadian nurse stamp of 1958 caused a national scandal, when it was disclosed that the model was a secretary. Outraged nurses throughout Canada demanded to know if the government thought no nurses were pretty enough to be pictured.

Stamps issued to honor the nursing profession cover the range of their professional and volunteer services. At one time, most of the nursing stamps focused on war. Now, war is out, pediatrics is in, and a great many of the present-day nursing stamps deal with pediatrics, which as a specialty forms the largest category of nursing stamp designs. The new nations of Africa and Asia are particularly prone to this design, and hardly a year goes by without a number of bold and modern designs issuing from the two continents.

In many other designs the nurse is symbolic, but the symbolic design is giving way to reality and the new nursing stamps being issued favor depicting a real nurse performing her duties. Some show her giving an IV or blood transfusion, assisting a surgeon, bandaging a child, or aiding the blind and crippled.

Some countries have issued a large number of nursing stamps. Turkey, with over 90 such stamps, is the undisputed leader. Albania, Latvia, Afghanistan, Haiti, and Hungary have each issued from 20 to 30. Belgium, Rumania, Estonia, Ethiopia, Germany and Jugoslavia have issued from 10 to 20 each.

Incidentally, male nurses have not been omitted from stampic honors. In 1964, Austria issued a stamp to mark the three hundred and fiftieth anniversary of the Brothers of Mercy. It shows one of the brothers caring for a patient.

37. Petroleum Industry

Petroleum has received much recognition for its contributions to human progress, but the most consistent bestower of honor is the postage stamp. More than 80 countries have issued almost 1000 stamps honoring the oil industry and its services.

A collection of oil stamps can be put together to display the history of the industry since the discovery of oil in Titusville, Pennsylvania, in 1859. A few carefully selected pages of oil stamps would just about cover the entire process of bringing oil from the ground to its many uses around the world.

One would see a map of an Arabian desert dotted with oil derricks, the pipelines of Iran, an early oil lamp of the 90's, and the many industrial uses of oil which fuels cars, trucks, railroads, and airplanes. There would be booming cities in the wastelands which spring up and are sustained by the nearby oil fields, the organic chemical and petrochemical industries, and, of course, the men who pioneered in new development and uses for oil.

The first known oil stamps were issued in 1919 by the then autonomous Soviet province of Azerbaijan. They show oil derricks of the Bibi Eibatt oil field and temples of the primitive fire worshippers where gas veins fed ancient fires of the Persian temples.

The leader in oil stamp issues today is Romania, home of the great Ploesti oil fields, with some 140 issues. Venezuela runs a distant second with 80 releases.

The United States, which consumes most of the world's oil, has issued only four oil stamps. In 1940 it issued a 3-cent commemorative of the fiftieth anniversary of the admission of Wyoming to statehood. It shows the word "oil," in the listing of the state's natural treasures. The 1950 California centennial stamp shows oil derricks in the background, and the 1951 issue to commemorate the seventy-fifth anniversary of the American Chemical Society shows a catalytic plant. On August 27, 1959, a 4-cent commemorative was issued in honor of the petroleum industry's centennial. It shows the Drake well at Titusville, Pa.

Canada has issued five oil stamps. In 1950, a 50-center was issued to publicize the development of oil in Canada. It shows an oil derrick, tanks, and an oil well fire in Alberta. In 1955, a commemorative issued for the fiftieth anniversary of the founding of the provinces of Alberta and Saskatchewan shows oil derricks in the background of a stylized farm scene. An unusual oil stamp is the 5-cent value of 1958 issued to commemorate the centennial of the oil industry: It shows a kerosene lamp and a refinery, each outlined in a drop of oil. Canada's latest entry is a double in the pictorial set of 1967-1970. The 3-cent stamp shows an oil derrick in the background of a farm scene and the set's high value, the $1, reproduces "Oilfield," a painting by H. G. Glyde, of an oilfield near Edmonton.

It's a task to find a country that hasn't issued an oil stamp. Hungary issued one in 1962, in honor of the twenty-fifth anniversary of its discovery of oil. Netherland Antilles issued a colorful set of stamps to mark the fiftieth anniversary of the oil industry in Curacao. Even Madagascar, a fairly new entry in the oil industry, honored it with a set of stamps issued in 1962.

Many countries issue stamps showing the routes of their pipelines. A complete collection of oil stamps would show most of the sources of oil and the pipelines that carry it to ports and refineries.

In 1961, Poland issued a stamp showing a map of Central and Eastern Europe. On it, red lines detail the route of the great Russian pipeline to Germany and Czechoslovakia across Poland, Romania, and Hungary. This pipeline system originating in Western Siberia is some 2700 miles long and with more than 20 pumping stations is one of the largest crude oil pipeline systems in the world.

New developments in oil technology quickly find their way onto postage stamps.

In 1969, Dubai issued a set of five stamps portraying the construction of the world's first underwater oil storage tank. The colorful, bold stamps show the construction and the launching of the tank, and the tank as installed. Many of the recent Middle East stamps are remarkable for their bold and modern designs.

Scientists who pioneered in oil technology have also been honored on stamps. Paul Sabatier, Nobel Prize winner for catalytic chemistry, is shown on a French stamp of 1956. A 1960 stamp issued by Poland honors Ignacy Lukasiewicz, who first distilled kerosene from oil and used it for lighting.

Oil world financiers and executives have not been omitted from the stampic honors. Andrew Mellon (an oil company president) is shown on one of the Famous American stamps, and John D. Rockefeller was selected for a stamp by the government of Belgium. In 1965, Portugal honored the legendary Calouste Gulbenkian who became immensely wealthy acting as a go-between in putting together the Iraq Petroleum Company (5 percent royalty for life).

Outstanding collections of oil stamps have been made by philatelists, many of them oil executives and field workers who became interested in the hobby. To help interested beginners in oil stamp collecting, French oilman Jean Barbedette (4 Rue Nicolet, Paris 18e) has formed the Friends of Petroleum, a group of oil stamp collectors world wide who exchange stamps and help newcomers get started. One of their members has put together a 50-page check list of oil stamps and another has published a book on the subject. If you're interested in joining, they'll welcome your letter.

38. Pharmacy and the Pharmaceutical Industry

The first country to honor the pharmaceutical industry philatically was Costa Rica, when a stamp depicting the industry was included in a series of stamps honoring the various essential Costa Rican industries. In 1964, both the Republic of China (Taiwan) and the People's Republic of China issued stamps publicizing their pharmaceutical industries. The Taiwan stamp shows the testing of drugs, while the Peking issue pictures the filling of ampules for injectable drugs.

In 1967, Poland issued a commemorative postcard honoring the twentieth anniversary of the Polish pharmaceutical industry. The following year Brazil honored Orlando de Fonseca Rangel, pioneer of the pharmaceutical industry in that country. In 1970, U.A.R. (Egypt) issued a stamp commemorating the thirtieth anniversary of the production of medicines in Egypt.

Pharmaceutical conferences of various types have been honored with commemorative stamps and/or special commemorative cancellations. The Fifth Scientific Pharmaceutical Congress held in Poznan, Poland, in 1960, was the occasion of the issuance of a Polish stamp in honor of Ignacy Lukasiewicz, the Polish pharmacist who first distilled kerosene from oil and used it for lighting. The Federation of Asian Pharmaceutical Associations (FAPA) was honored with a Korean stamp in 1968. Two years later, the Philippines commemorated the 1970 FAPA Congress and Fiftieth Anniversary of the Philippine Pharmaceutical Association.

Several stamps exist which depict manufactured drugs. A 1963 Hungarian stamp shows a child with medicines, while one of the 1971 stamps of Ghana, issued for the International Fair, shows various medications within its design. A 1973 stamp of North Korea shows drugs as export products, while the recent series of Qatar, issued for the twenty-fifth anniversary of the World Health Organization, includes a stamp titled "Drug Healing."

Pharmaceutical tools have been depicted on stamps of Korea and Japan issued for the changeover to the metric systems. Drug jars

of the monastic period, called *albarellos*, are shown on Portuguese stamps of 1964. In 1970, an early mortar and pestle and two sixteenth-century Italian drug jars appeared on a stamp of Malta.

Pharmacy was first honored with a stamp in 1927, when a set of three stamps was issued by Poland on the occasion of the Fourth International Congress of Military Medicine and Pharmacy held in Warsaw. Poland, incidentally, has issued a number of postal items in honor of pharmacy, including several postcards.

The first "pure" pharmacy stamp was issued by Cuba in 1948, to commemorate the First Pan American Congress of Pharmacy at Havana. Another Cuban stamp, issued in 1957 to publicize the Jose Marti National Library in Havana, shows the first Cuban publication, a price list of drugs printed in Cuba in 1723. Other pharmacy stamps include the striking design of the U.S. pharmacy stamp, issued in 1972. In 1971, Czechoslovakia issued a stunning set of six stamps on the occasion of the International Congress of the History of Pharmacy held in Prague. The stamps show ancient medicinal plants and early pharmacy equipment.

Despite the many stamps issued with the pharmacy motif, only four are known to picture the pharmacist at work. In 1939, Belgium issued a stamp depicting the interior of a medieval monastic pharmacy. One monk is studying a manuscript while a second grinds drugs in his mortar. A 1222 Islamic miniature titled "The Dispensary" or *La Pharmacie* was reproduced on a 1967 stamp of the Mutawakelite Kingdom of Yemen, one from a series of stamps showing early Arabic manuscript illustrations. The third "working pharmacist" stamp will be mentioned later on, and the fourth stamp is a 1971 miniature from Ajman. The stamp reproduces a painting called *"Lo Speziale"* (The Pharmacist) painted by Pietro Loghi (1702-1785). It shows the interior of an Italian country pharmacy with the physician seated at the table writing a prescription and

the pharmacist administering the ordered remedy to the patient.

While "visible" pharmacy has been largely slighted by postal authorities, its famous practitioners and those who made notable contributions to it have been honored on the stamps of many nations.

The man honored by most countries is the famous Italian poet Dante Alighieri. Dante was a member of the guild of physicians and apothecaries of Florence. His family owned two pharmacies in that city, one of which, the *Farmacia del Canto alle Rondini,* is still in business, now the oldest in the city.

Another widely honored personage is Abn' al Hussain Ibn' Abdullah Ibn Sina Efschene, also known as Avicenna. One of the greatest of Arab philosophers and physicians, he is best known for his *Canon of Medicine,* a five-volume work that became the basis for uncompromising medical doctrine in the Middle Ages. The fifth book describes the composition and preparation of remedies. He is on a 1948 stamp of Lebanon which pictures him preparing some medical concoction. This is one of the four stamps in the world depicting the actual work of a pharmacist.

Two renowned pharmacists, whose names are almost invariably linked, are Pierre-Joseph Pelletier and Joseph-Bienaimé Caventou. Both came from families well-established in French pharmaceutical circles. Their fathers were both pharmacists and Pelletier's grandfather was also a master apothecary. Neither made much profit from the discovery of quinine, but it assured them of immortality, for they gave their process for the preparation of quinine sulphate to the world. They are depicted on a stamp of France issued in 1970 for the one hundred and fiftieth anniversary of the great discovery.

Benjamin Franklin is one of several American pharmacy personages depicted on United States stamps. From 1730 to 1749 he sold drugs and patent medicines in his shop in Philadelphia and in 1952 was instrumental in the opening of the apothecary shop in the Pennsylvania Hospital, one of the first steps in separation of pharmacy from medicine in this country. Harvey W. Wiley, chemist and physician, whose efforts led to the enactment of the United States Pure Food and Drug Laws in 1906, was honored on a stamp issued in 1956 for the fiftieth anniversary of the passage of the laws.

Two American pharmacists honored by foreign countries are former Vice-President Hubert H. Humphrey, and the well-known writer, O. Henry (pen name of William Sydney Porter). Humphrey, son of a pharmacist, started his career as a pharmacist and still retains his license in South Dakota. He is shown on a 1964 stamp of Ajman. O. Henry, who was a pharmacist by profession (licensed in North Carolina), is on a stamp of Russia issued in 1962.

One of the most distinguished pharmacists honored on stamps is Carl Wilhelm Scheele, one of the greatest chemists of all time. After serving an eight-year apothecary apprenticeship in Gothenburg, he worked in Malmo, Stockholm, and Uppsala. In 1775, he became proprietor of his own pharmacy in Koping. He had a habit of tasting and smelling all substances he handled and one of these tasting exercises induced a rheumatic attack which in turn led to his death in 1786.

The long gallery of pharmacy personages on stamps includes Chinese pharmacologist Li Che-Tchen, whose 1578 medical treatise *Pen ts'ao kang mou* describes almost 2000 remedies and over 8000 prescriptions; Sir Isaac Newton, whose first job was in a local apothecary shop in Woolsthrope; Jons Jakon Berzelius, "father of gravimetric analysis," who was a professor of pharmacy and botany at the University of Stockholm; the world's first balloonist (1783), Jean Joseph Pilatre de Rozier, who was a pharmaceutical apprentice and pharmacy student; ancient Chinese pharmacist and alchemist Souen Sseu-Mo, author of *Ts' ien-chin i-fang* or "Thousand Precious Prescriptions" (circa 600 A.D.); Jean Pierre Mickelers, Dutch pharmacist, who first used gas from coal for lighting, and many others.

39. Police

At least 75 nations have issued stamps in honor of their police forces or illustrating police activities. Policemen (and women) and related subjects have appeared on more stamps than may be realized, and many issues, especially in recent years, have included some attractive stamps.

The first stamp to portray a policeman was a 1932 issue of Papua, depicting Sergeant Major Simoi of the Papua Constabulary. But prior to this, in 1893, El Salvador issued a stamp showing their president, General Ezete, wearing a helmet identical to those worn by British policemen. This stamp might be considered as an interesting introductory novelty in a collection of police stamps.

Other early police stamps include an El Salvador issue of 1934 which shows Police Headquarters and an Italian stamp of the same year with an Italian *Carabinier.* In 1935, Canada issued the first of its stamps to honor the Royal Canadian Mounted Police (another one was issued in 1973); Turkey issued a stamp showing a policewoman for the Twelfth Congress, International Women's Alliance; and Guatemala depicted its police headquarters. Guatemala issued a police stamp in 1935, and two more in 1937; Fiji joined the postal gallery in 1938, Southern Rhodesia in 1940, and Gold Coast in 1948.

The 1930s and 1940s saw only a small number of police stamps. More were issued during the 1950s, and the 1960s, when the subject finally came into its own as a stamp design. The American police stamp, the "Law and Order" issue, was issued in 1967.

Russia, where the police are very "visible," has issued police stamps since 1964. Russian stamps have honored public security Militiamen, the Frontier Guards, and the infamous secret police, the K.G.B.

Curiously enough Nazi Germany issued only one police stamp, in 1939, and that depicted Postal Police, being one out of a set issued to salute German postal employees. West Germany issued a police stamp in 1956, on the occasion of the International Police Exhibition in Essen. They also have issued several traffic safety stamps showing police activities. East Germany has also issued a number of traffic safety stamps as well as a series of five stamps in 1970 for the twenty-fifth anniversary of the founding of the People's Police. This set includes stamps showing a policewoman, railroad police, and river police.

Traffic safety is the police activity most often shown on stamps. The subject of traffic safety as a stamp design has gained great popularity during the past few years, and a number of interesting stamps on this subject have appeared from around the globe.

Global crime fighting has been saluted by stamps of 28 nations issued in 1973 for the fiftieth anniversary of the International Criminal Police Organization, more popularly known as INTERPOL.

Many of these nation's tributes consist of picturing the INTERPOL emblem or the headquarters building in Paris. Other designs show radio operators and radio waves; detectives and fingerprints; criminal evidence; and one set, from Nicaragua, depicts 12 fictional detectives, from novels, radio, TV, and the movies.

Other police stamps include athletes who have been identified as policemen, postmarks used by police postal agencies, stamps overprinted especially for use by police forces, and many other similar items one becomes aware of once one starts to collect police stamps.

40. Railroads

Despite the fact that millions of collectors eagerly pursue the thousands of colorful commemorative stamps issuing from all the world's postal authorities, only a very few of them know that the world's first commemorative stamp was issued in honor of a railroad and includes a locomotive in its design.

This "father" of today's flood of stamps is a small, five centavos scarlet stamp of Peru, issued in April of 1871 to commemorate the twentieth anniversary of the first railroad in South America, built by the Peruvian field marshall D. Ramon Castilla, linking the capital city of Lima with its seaport, Callao, and a fancy seaside resort, Chorrillos. A locomotive and a coat of arms form its design.

Since Peru's 0-6-0 Steam Engine first graced postal paper, over 4500 "railroad stamps" have been issued by some 260 countries, including many nations and colonies that no longer exist. There is something for everybody in this postal gallery, in which you can find all kinds of engines— steam, electric, diesel, and turbine—tracks, signals, bridges, tunnels, stations, gandy dancers, and even toy trains.

Many stamps have been issued merely to illustrate various engines, and quite a few of them have been identified either on the stamps themselves or by expert railroaders who are collectors. Despite the advent of the jet age and the conquest of space, the locomotive remains a world-wide favorite as a stamp design. Recent modernistic sets of locomotive stamps from the various African countries, which are now entering the era of railroads, have been eagerly purchased by collectors. Most European nations, particularly those of Eastern Europe, regularly issue stamp sets showing engines, and even the United States which hardly "pushes" its railroads these days, issued a Christmas stamp, in 1970, depicting a toy locomotive.

The first United States railroad stamp was issued in 1869, depicting a 4-4-0 Steam Engine. Since then, at least a dozen locomotives have appeared on its stamps, most of them identified either by type or by name or number. The 4-4-0 Steam Engine #938 and passenger cars of The New York Central & Hudson River Railroad's "Empire State Express," appear on the 2-cent stamp of the 1901 Pan-American Exposition Issue. The Steam Engine "Jupiter" in the painting "Golden Spike Ceremony," by John

McQuarrie, is on the 1944 commemorative of the seventy-fifth anniversary of the completion of the first transcontinental railroad.

The next identified engine— or rather two of them— is on the 1950 Railroad Engineers Issue depicting engineer "Casey" Jones. On the left is a 1900 4-6-0 Steam Engine #382; on the right are a 1950 Diesel Engine and passenger cars of the Illinois Central Railroad.

The one hundred and twenty-fifth anniversary of the granting of a charter to the Baltimore and Ohio Railroad by the Maryland Legislature was commemorated with a stamp in 1952. The design, showing three stages of transportation, includes an 0-2-2 Steam Engine, "Tom Thumb," built in 1929 by Peter Cooper, and the B & O Railroad 1,500HP Diesel Engine, Type F3, built in 1947 by GM.

The only other identified engine on United States stamps is on the 1947 Postage Stamp Centenary Issue which shows various early and modern mail-carrying vehicles. One is a 4-4-0 Steam Engine and the other a Diesel Engine.

Various locomotives have also been depicted on the stamps issued by the United States Post Office for use in the Canal Zone. One can be identified. It's on a stamp issued in 1955 and it's a 4-4-0 Steam Engine, "Nueva Granada," built in the U.S. in 1852.

Other railroading designs include crossing gates and signs, mining railways (at least 60 different stamps), railroad stations, signals, tracks and rails, tunnels, and allegorical designs, such as, for example, winged wheels. Canal railways (for towing ships through a canal) appear on stamps that Panama and the United States issued for the Canal Zone. Six countries have issued stamps showing railroad car ferries. Monorails appear on stamps of Romania, Russia, and the United States, while accidents and wrecks are depicted by Cuba, Mexico, and Russia— the last a prolific issuer of all kinds of railroad stamps.

Cars— passenger, mail, freight, and work— are another popular design and over 90 countries have issued stamps showing bridges or viaducts, while at least 25 have depicted cranes on rails on some 55 stamps. Railroad workers (construction, operations, maintenance, etc.), are on stamps of at least 45 countries, with the largest number of such stamps issued by Russia, Hungary, and Belgium. Belgium, which issues special "Parcel Post and Railway" stamps, is the world's undisputed leader in the gallery, with over 400 stamps issued.

The events that called for the issuance of the many stamps are varied. Besides those issued as mere pictorials, others were issued for parcel post service, for centenaries of the various railroads (a whole collection of centenaries can be put together), for various less-than-centenary anniversaries, for projects involving railway constructions, for openings of bridges and rail services, for meetings, congresses, and anniversaries of organizations (such as, for example the fiftieth anniversary of the UIC, the International Railroad Union), and even for the promotion of tourism.

41. Scouting

Most Scouts and Scouters are interested in many phases of stamp collecting and in stamps from all countries, but many of them are particularly interested in stamps related to their own organization and its many sided activities.

Those interested in forming a collection of Scout stamps will find many informative articles on this subject, several books, and a collectors' society devoted to collecting only Scouting stamps— Scouts on Stamps Society International.

The first Scout stamps are older than Scouting itself. They were issued in 1900, during the 219-day siege of Mafeking in South Africa, during the Boer War. There, the British garrison, commanded by Col. Robert Baden-Powell, successfully fought off a much stronger Boer force. Boys were organized into a Cadet Corps to provide local bicycle mail service and it was from his experience with this group that Baden-Powell developed the Scouting idea.

As there were no stamps available in Mafeking, two designs were produced by photography. One portrayed Col. Baden-Powell, the other depicted Cadet Sergeant Major Warner Goodyear— later called "the first Scout"—riding his bicycle. Today, these stamps are quite expensive and actual covers (some were carried by native runners through enemy lines) are rare and valuable.

The first stamp to picture a Boy Scout was issued by Hungary in 1925 as part of a set of stamps depicting various sports. These stamps were surcharged (carried an additional price) for the benefit of various athletic and youth groups. The additional price collected on the Scout stamp went to the Hungarian Boy Scouts.

Hungary was also the first country to issue stamps in honor of a World Scout Jamboree. This was in 1933, when Hungary hosted the Fourth World Jamboree at Godollo. The stamps proved so popular that since that time Scout stamps have been issued by every Jamboree host nation. In 1957, Britain issued a set of three stamps to commemorate the Golden Jubilee of Scouting, which coincided with the Ninth World Jamboree in Sutton Coldfield (where the Scouting movement was launched) and the one hundredth anniversary of the birth of Lord Baden-Powell. There were Scout stamps issued from other nations complimenting the fiftieth anniversary of Scouting and since then it has been usual for a World Jamboree to inspire Scout stamp issues by more than the host

country. In 1967, for example, some 15 countries issued Scout stamps to commemorate the Twelfth World Jamboree, and more than a dozen nations honored the Thirteenth World Jamboree in 1971.

The World Jamboree commemorative stamps are only a small fraction of Scout stamps issued around the globe. Many countries have issued stamps for their national jamborees. The United States' first Boy Scout stamp was issued in connection with the Second National Jamboree held in 1950 in Valley Forge, Pennsylvania. Other issues have honored regional gatherings—such as, for example, the 1948 Pan-Pacific Jamboree in Wonga Park, Australia—and there are many Scout stamps which were issued for anniversaries of Scouting in various countries. A number of stamps exist commemorating the centenary of the birth of Baden-Powell.

New Scout stamps are issued each year by many countries. In 1973, for example, 21 countries issued over 90 Scouting stamps!

There are also stamps issued for the Girl Guides and Girl Scouts and some have also pictured their founder, Lady Baden-Powell, who has carried on as a vital force in the Scouting movement since the death of her husband in 1941.

In addition to Scouting stamps there are many First Day covers of the commemorative stamps, many decorative cachets, and a number of special commemorative cancellations for the various Scouting events.

42. Ships

Since the world's first postage stamp was issued by England in 1840, some 12,000 stamps have depicted some watercraft in their design. In fact, the ship is one of the world's earliest stamp designs, dating back to 1852, when sailing ships first decorated the stamps of British Guiana. Fittingly, the world's rarest stamp, the British Guiana 1-cent magenta of 1856, depicts a sailing ship. This famous stamp last changed hands at a public auction in New York for the fantastic sum of $280,000!

The huge number of watercraft stamps are matched with a variety of designs which allows any interest to build a fine collection. Whether passenger liners, submarines, junks, battleships, oil tankers, canoes, or yachts, there is an ample supply of material available—and plenty of information in the form of articles and books. There is even available a check list of some 1100 vessels on stamps which have been identified by name, some officially, others by sharp-eyed collectors. There is plenty of room for discoveries by those who want to dig deep into history while forming their collections. For example, in 1969, a New York collector found an advertisement used in the early 1880s to promote S.S. Elbe, a passenger liner of the North German Lloyd. Armed with that photograph he was positively able to identify a ship on a stamp of Uruguay, issued in 1885, as the S.S. Elbe—the vessel's code flags provided positive identification!

There are many ways of forming a collection of ships on stamps. A common way is to use a type of vessel of individual interest; a submariner might collect postal subs; an ex-Antarctic explorer might want to collect only Antarctic vessels, and divide them into ages of sail, steam, and oil. Others collect battleships, yachts, or cable-laying vessels. Passenger liners of certain ship lines have been made into collections, and cargo ships can be collected in their different categories. Fishing vessels are particularly prominent here, with almost every type represented, including the modern factory ships.

Of the various broad subjects, an excellent collection can be built depicting sailing ships. Today, the conquest of space and its heroes are being honored with thousands of stamps of all nations, but even that fails to stem the flow of hundreds of stamps issued in honor of man's most romantic achievement, the conquest of the seas. The sailing ship, the "space ship" of yesterday, continues to appear regularly, proof of the pride that sea-faring nations still feel for those explorers, and proof that countries which couldn't take part in that conquest still feel the importance of its impact on their modern history. Almost a complete history of sailing and the conquest of the seas can be shown with a collection of sailing stamps— and it does not need to cost too much if you apply yourself to the project.

A collection of just American stamps showing watercraft can be a challenging project. Over 150 of these have been issued since 1869 and there are also some American ships on foreign stamps. Some of the foreign stamps also show warships of American origin, whose names have been changed after they were sold or traded. (Once a warship has been identified, it's not difficult to trace its origin.) Another facet of an Americana collection of ships are foreign liners which regularly served United States ports. In addition to stamps, there exists a wealth of special postmarks and cachets used for different marine events, particularly for maiden voyages. Also, there are cancels of ships' post offices— all material to dress-up the collection.

Shipbuilding is another interesting field in which to build a collection. The United States issued a shipbuilding stamp in 1957 and many other nations have depicted the building of various types of vessels on their stamps. There are probably at least 100 stamps showing a vessel being constructed, some by hand, by island natives in the Pacific, others in modern docks. Naval shipyards and individual craftsmen are also on stamps; there is even a stamp which shows the plan of a vessel.

Even a relatively small subject can be built into a prize-winning collection. This was done a few years ago with submarines. This is the scarcest of all warship motifs and only about 35 stamps exist with a sub in their design. Yet, an ex-submariner was able to build a prize-winning collection by digging into the backgrounds, identifying the vessels, and locating interesting facts about them. This easily proves that it is not the number of stamps available in your field of interest which makes for a good collection, but how you approach the project— and how much you know about your subject. Battleships are another excellent collection subject with a number of American ships on stamps available. There also exists a stamp of Japan which shows the U.S. fleet at Pearl Harbor at the time of the attack.

Most sea-bordering nations, the island nations in particular, have issued hundreds of stamps depicting their particular native small craft. An interesting collection of these vessels could be formed, accompanied by photographs, if wanted, and described in detail after some study of the different types of vessels. There are such craft there as junks, sampans, dugouts with outriggers, the Figian "takia" and the "wangga vakata," the Maori canoes, and the Tonga longboats, to name just a few. The choices are there, whatever watercraft you fancy.

43. Space Exploration

The exploration and conquest of space is the world's most popular stamp collecting topic.

Normally, nations honor their own glories and native sons on their postage, but worthy foreigners and events reflecting directly or indirectly on the history or welfare of a country are also often commemorated with stamp issues. Many nations have honored great men and epic events. The discovery of the New York by Columbus, the Russian Revolution, the founding of the United Nations, the death of President Kennedy— all of these have been honored by hundreds of stamps issued by various nations. But the event most often depicted on postage stamps is the exploration and conquest of space.

Probably more stamps have been issued to depict the many steps in man's conquest of space than have been issued to honor all the important events in mankind's history put together. More are issued each year; every step forward in the conquest of the unknown outer world is honored by a stamp from *some* nation, for almost every country in the world has issued a "space stamp" of one kind or another.

Space stamps come in many forms. There are not only those issued to commemorate actual flights—manned, unmanned, or exploratory to other planets— but they include many issues depicting satellites and satellite communications. There are rocketry stamps (forerunners of space) and there are stamps honoring the various scientists and pioneers in technology who made important contributions to the current conquest of space.

The United States Post Office has issued several "pure" space stamps, including the large 10-cent air mail for the first moon landing and the spectacular 1967 "double": two 5-cent stamps of different designs side by side, one showing space-walking astronauts and the other Gemini 4 capsule and the earth.

A collection of "pure" space stamps—those covering actual flights into space to the exclusion of communication satellites, personalities, and rockets— could document complete space history. The first space stamp was issued by Russia in 1957 to commemorate the launching of the first artificial earth satellite, October 4, 1957. Since then, Russia has issued a stamp for its every space effort. Sputniks, space dogs, cosmonauts, interplanetary vehicles, and space

probes have appeared in a dazzling variety.

Russian space efforts have been hailed by many other nations. Naturally, the satellite nations have commemorated a great many of the Soviet space achievements, but honors were also accorded to some American space achievements—the first time ever that politically opposed nations have honored the achievements of an adversary. Neutral countries have honored both the Soviet and the American steps in the conquest of space. A great many stamps have been issued depicting the various Soviet unmanned interplanetary vehicles and space probes which excite the imagination with the promise of further space exploration during our lifetimes. The sole space lady, Valentina Tereschkowa, has had her share of honors. Her most unusual stamp, a "double" from East Germany, is illustrated in the photo plate.

A wealth of other philatelic material is available to the space stamp collector. There are covers signed by the astronauts, some very highly prized, and there are many special commemorative cancellations and cachets on covers specially prepared for the many space-related events. There are also covers from the recovery ships, flown covers, and many interesting Russian space cancellations. Several books have been written, listing the enormous amount of the varied materials available to space collectors.

44. Sports

The choice of postal-paper sports is large. The great, world-wide interest in the Olympics, the revival of bicycling, and the emphasis on physical fitness have combined to catapult sports on stamps to the top of the list of the favorite stamp collecting topics.

The interest in sport stamps collecting has not been lost on the postal administration, as can be seen by the issuance of many stamps depicting sports previously rarely used as stamp motifs. Skin diving, for example, seldom seen on stamps in the past, is now an accepted stamp design, and a sufficient number of them have been issued to make it a collectible topic. Other "new" sports on stamps are judo, water skiing, parachuting, bobsledding, and golf.

The revival of the bicycle is adding dozens of new bicycle sport stamps to the gallery every year. The United States 1972 Olympic set of four stamps included a bike stamp, and the majority of Olympic stamp sets issued that year contained a bike stamp. A large and interesting collection of these can be built with a reasonable expenditure. Bicycling is very popular in Eastern Europe and many stamp sets are issued every year by those countries to publicize various local and international racing events.

The afficionado of ping-pong, or table ten-

nis, can add the many Red Chinese ping-pong stamps to his collection. Japan has also issued a number of them and many Japanese table tennis events have been commemorated with special pictorial cancellations which are very interesting as a collection. Many countries have issued ping-pong stamps and most of them are remarkable for their accuracy of design.

Tennis is an old sports stamp motif and though the United States itself has never issued a tennis stamp, the world's first tennis stamp was issued in 1934 by the United States Post Office for use in the Philippines, which were administered at that time by the United States. Tennis stamps have been issued by a large number of countries and recently many of them have appeared forming part of sets issued to publicize tourism.

By far the most popular of all sports motifs is the general topic of the Olympics. More stamps have been issued for the Olympic games than for all the other sport events together. One is hard-pressed to think of a country which has *not* issued Olympic stamps regardless of whether or not it participated in the Games.

Olympic stamps date back to the first Modern Olympiad, held in Athens in 1896. The event was commemorated by a set of 12

Greek stamps depicting scenes from the Ancient Games. The United States has issued a total of eight Olympic stamps: one for the 1932 Winter Games at Lake Placid; two for the Tenth Olympiad at Los Angeles (1932); one for the Eighth Winter Games at Squaw Valley in 1960; and the four for the 1972 Games in Munich.

At least 50 nations have issued ski stamps and this topic is steadily growing in popularity. One favorite design of the ski stamps issued for the Olympics is the rifleman (biathlon), which is also properly suited for inclusion in a collection of shooting stamps.

Shooting has been an Olympic event since the first Modern Olympiad (which included a free pistol event) and it has been depicted on a small but collectible gallery of stamps. Both pistol and rifle shooting are shown on stamps and there are a small number of stamps which depict just the weapons. Archery, of course, is a very popular sport and a great many stamps have been issued with that motif.

Skating is well represented in the gallery with a number of striking designs having been issued for the Winter Games at Sapporo. A number of stamps also exist showing dancing on skates.

Other individual sports well illustrated on stamps, and suitable as collection material, are boxing, fencing, weight lifting, wrestling, swimming, gliding, rowing, sailing, and, of course, all gymnastics and track and field events.

45. Telephone and Telecommunications

The first stamp picturing a telephone instrument was issued by Germany in 1934. The United States, though it leads the world in number of telephones, has never shown one on a stamp, but it did issue a stamp for the 1965 centenary of the International Telecommunications Union, an occasion that called for all kinds of interesting-looking stamps to be issued around the world.

Very few telecommunications stamps existed prior to 1950, when the subject suddenly came into vogue and telephones and other paraphernalia of telecommunications began to appear on postal paper as more and more stamps were issued in honor of communications-connected events. These events became more frequent in the 1950s than before. Europe, recovered from World War II, was entering an era of prosperity; the new nations emerging in Africa were entering the world arena very much aware of the importance of proper telephone service, and communications everywhere were improving rapidly, with the telephone— aided by the telecommunications satellites— becoming commonplace throughout the world.

Once the subject of telecommunications became an accepted stamp motif, designers vied with each other to make the stamps more interesting and striking. The telephone instrument became the object of artistic efforts to present it as strikingly as possible. Some stamps show the entire instrument— sometimes modern, sometimes antique— others portray people speaking into the handset, or maybe just the handset itself. A series of stamps issued by Rwanda in 1965, in memory of President Kennedy, shows him speaking into a telephone handset. The dial of the telephone became the object of various stamp designs, some very unusual. When Luxembourg changed to the dial telephone system in 1963, it issued a stamp showing a symbolic map of the country with stars showing locations of major telephone exchanges and a dial in the center of the map. Another interesting dial stamp was issued by Japan in 1965. Its whole design is the dial, with the picture of an 1890 switchboard replacing the phone number. International subscriber dialing was honored with a symbolic dial on a British stamp of 1969.

Communications satellites appeared on

postal paper in full array, and cable-laying ships sailed onto stamps in reasonable numbers. Transmitting and receiving antennas, radio sine waves, telephone operators, linemen repairing the wires, telephone exchange buildings, and various symbolic designs (including the ITU symbol of a bolt of lightning—the initials shown on stamps are UIT, for the official designation in French of *L'Union Internationale des Télécommunications*) appeared around the globe to the delight of stamp collectors interested in telecommunications.

Perhaps the most striking telephone stamp is the one issued by Tunisia in 1962 to commemorate the automatization of the telephone system. It shows a symbolic telephone man or woman. His head is the dial of a telephone, his arm holds a handset to his ear, and his body is made up of complex switching equipment. Another unusual stamp is the Guatemalan Red Cross issue of 1956, showing a red cross with a telephone in the center. Rays of light reach from the telephone to number 5110 at the lower right, the telephone number of the Red Cross in Guatemala. An outline of a telephone enclosing a map of Southeast Asia and Australia forms the design of a stamp issued by Hong Kong in 1967 to commemorate the completion of the Hong Kong-Malaysia link of Southeast Asia Commonwealth Cable, SEACOM. The world's only triangular telephone stamp was issued by the Trucial States sheikdom of Sharjah; it shows an early telephone instru-

ment. A modern push-button telephone instrument forms the design of an East German stamp issued to publicize the 1970 Leipzig Spring Fair.

The 1965 celebration of the centenary of the International Telecommunications Union resulted in many commemorative stamps issued around the world. Many of these included a telephone in the design. Some of the nations of the French community took this opportunity to show on their stamps interesting old telephones. The Senegal design shows a French-made Berton-Ader Magneto telephone. An Ader telephone is shown on the stamp of Niger, and another model of it is pictured by Dahomey. An ancient Mildé instrument is shown by Chad. Another stamp in this category deserves mention. It was issued in 1961 to commemorate the centenary of the invention of the Reis telephone by Philipp Reis, whom the Germans claim to be the inventor of the telephone. His instrument, shown on the stamp, was not a success. The ancient telephone that *was* a sucess, and its inventor, Alexander Graham Bell, are shown on the 1965 UIT commemorative of Monaco. Bell is also on stamps of Canada and the United States.

Switchboard operators are on stamps of a number of nations. A battery of busy operators manning a central switchboard appears on a stamp of Czechoslovakia, issued in 1958. There are many others.

46. Textile Industry

The textile industry was one of the world's first industries, dating back to the times of the Egyptian Pharaohs, and every phase of it has been depicted on postage stamps.

Stamps from most of the world's nations depict textile fibers, plants and animals that produce them, power and handlooms, spinning wheels, bobbins and shuttles, and textile mills. Others show products of the industry—fabrics, tapestries, laces, and rugs. Yet others display fashions, native costumes, and the needles, thread, and sewing machines that make them. Textile stamps can form a collection covering either the whole industry or a particular phase of it.

Recently, some very interesting, ingenious, and bold designs have appeared in this category. A 1970 stamp of Finland, issued to publicize its textile industry, features swatches in the shapes of factories. A shuttle forms the central design of a French stamp issued in 1951 to publicize the International Textile Exposition at Lille, while an allegory of textile manufacture is the design of the Belgian stamp of 1955, issued to publicize the second International Textile Exhibition at Brussels. Belgium has issued many excellent textile designs. One issued in 1965 shows a montage of various symbols of the industry. It was issued for the "Textrama" textile industry exhibition at Ghent.

Russia has issued a large number of stamps for the industry, many of them indicating the progress that is being made in textile production. A typical Russian design is the 1964 issue to publicize the importance of the textile industry in the Russian economy. Such "symbolic" textile stamps have been issued by at least 20 nations.

Some of the best textile stamp designs are being issued by the newly emerging nations, who take great pride in showing their new industries to the world via postage stamps. An unusual design, in very attractive colors, was used in 1971 by Upper Volta to publicize its industrial development. It shows cotton and the emblem of the local Voltex mill. Cloth color printing is depicted on a textile industry stamp of the Ivory Coast, issued in 1970, one of a number of well-designed textile stamps issued by that small nation.

Fabrics are a very popular design of textile industry stamps. Fabrics are shown on a stamp of Israel, issued in 1968 as part of its series of various designs showing exports. Romania shows a woman showing a sample

of cloth on a 1962 stamp, issued for the Fourth Sample Fair at Bucharest, and women examining fabrics against a background of machinery are shown on stamps of East Germany and the People's Republic of China.

Collections of the various phases of the industry can be formed in an almost unlimited number of ways. Textile machinery is a very popular motif. Sometimes, the actual make of the machine has been identified by the issuing country; at other times it can be identified by a sharp-eyed expert forming his collection. One may even write a letter—or many letters!—to the postal authorities of the issuing nation and try to find out what make of equipment is shown. It's not easy, but it's part of the collecting game.

Equipment stamps include the automatic Diederich looms on a 1968 stamp of the Central African Republic and a circular knitting machine on a 1967 stamp of East Germany, issued to publicize the 1967 Leipzig Spring Fair. The spinnery of the SOTEXO textile plant at Kinsoundi is shown on a Congo stamp of 1970, while a similar design is used by the Republic of China for their textile industry stamp of 1964.

Textile mills—the buildings—can form another interesting collection; they have been shown on stamps of many nations, not necessarily the small ones. Russia, for example, produced a special stamp in 1957 to mark the centenary of the Krengholm textile works at Narva, Estonia. Textile personalities—the pioneers of the industry—can form a small collection. The United States has issued commemorative stamps for inventors Eli Whitney (cotton gin) and Elias Howe (sewing machine). Sweden has honored Jonas Alstromer, who established its first woolen mill; France issued a commemorative in 1955 for the inventor of rayon, Bernigaud de Chardonnet. Lesser known "textile" names—John Macarthur, G. Marzotto, Dayton Hedges, A. Rossi—might send one to the library to search through the encyclopedias.

Specific major divisions of the industry can also be shown with individual collections. The carpet industry can form a large collection, as can the wool industry—subject of hundreds of stamps. A recent one is the U.S. stamp of 1971, issued to commemorate the four hundred and fiftieth anniversary of the introduction of sheep to the North American continent and the beginning of the United States wool industry. The woolmark appears on a 1969 stamp of New Zealand; this is also a good candidate for a carpet industry collection, as the woolmark is shown on a carpet.

47. Trucks and the Trucking Industry

The importance of the trucking industry has been recently highlighted by several postage stamp issues from various countries. The 1973 set of United States "Postal People" stamps included a stamp titled "loading mail on a truck," showing the working end of a big semi. This was not the first time a government depicted trucking on stamps. The United States honored the trucking industry with a commemorative stamp back in 1953, on the occasion of the fiftieth anniversary of its trucking industry. The 1960 Wheels of Freedom stamp, issued in honor of the automotive industry, also included a heavy truck in its design. The role of the truck in postal service was recognized way back in 1925, when a Post Office truck was the design of the then Special Delivery stamp.

One need only look through the pages of a stamp catalog to see that the trucking industry has been widely honored around the world as a respectable and honorable profession and as an important economic factor.

The fact that the truck is a partner in the economy is clearly shown by the type of truck that is shown on various stamps. New Zealand, for example, is an important exporter of wool. Thus, a truck transporting bales of wool ap-pears on a stamp of that country. The lumber industry is very important in Paraguay, so it's only natural that her "March of Progress" stamps include one showing a truck moving logs.

The country which has issued the largest number of "truck" stamps is Russia. Over the years, all types of Russian trucks appeared on their stamps, depicting their use in various industries. In 1971, two big rigs appeared on a pair of unusual, triangular stamps issued to promote Russian truck exports. One stamp shows the Gaz 66; the other depicts the pride of the Russian trucking industry, the Belaz 540. This award-winning giant is available in pretty pastel colors, including yellow and blue.

Early in 1974, both Poland and Russia issued stamps showing trucks. The Polish set included two Polish-built heavy duty jobs, the Jelcz 316 and the Star 660. In the past, Poland issued an interesting stamp depicting the inside of a truck factory at Lublin. The new Russian stamp shows the first Soviet-built truck, the AMO-F15, which was produced beginning in 1924 by the Automobile Moscow Society.

The People's Republic of China has issued

several truck stamps. One, titled "truck," was issued in 1955, and another, showing trucks on the assembly line at Truck Factory No. 1 at Changchun, in 1957. Truck assembly is also shown on a stamp of Poland, issued in 1952, depicting the truck factory at Lublin.

Trucks are important export-import items and a number of stamps show them in that configuration. A semi is shown on a stamp of Ghana, issued in 1971 for the Second Ghana International Trade Fair, and Czech-made trucks appear on a stamp of 1958, one of a set issued to commemorate Czechoslovakia's motor industry. On the left is a Tatra 111, on the right, a Praga V3S. Both trucks are important exports and this stamp shows them "delivered" to far-off Tibet. The Tatra on the stamp has no windshield wipers, which means that the photo of the actual truck from which the design was made was not taken of a truck destined for Tibet, but of one ready for export to some country where it does not rain. (Vehicles used in desert climates work with wipers removed.)

The logging industry is shown on some excellent truck stamps. Shown here is a colorful stamp from Fiji, a large spectacular from the Cameroons, and a tiny stamp from Sweden. Another tiny stamp, from Rhodesia, shows a huge trailer rig transporting coffee bags. A triangular from the Congo shows another big rig, an unusual, pointy-nosed workhorse, and a box with a roof that is something "different." A trailer loaded with water pipes appears on a stamp of Guinea, one from a set issued to show the building of the Conakry aqueduct.

Mining and cement industries also account for a number of interesting truck stamp designs. The one shown here is from Mauritania and shows a dump truck being loaded with iron ore at the open pit mine at Zouerate.

Two recent trucking issues include one from Portugal in a set issued in 1972 to honor the Thirteenth Congress of International Union of Road Transport (I.R.U.) held at Estoril. The other is from Albania, also issued in 1972. It shows a large semi of unidentified make—it could be Chinese.

48. Veterinary Medicine

A mongrel dog—what could be more democratic?— is America's offical representative to the interesting gallery of postage stamps honoring the veterinary profession. Some 20 countries have issued about 40 stamps with some direct reference to veterinary medicine in their designs.

The American entry is the 5-cent Humane Treatment of Animals stamp issued in 1966 to commemorate the one hundredth anniversary of the founding of A.S.P.C.A. by Henry Bergh. The "official mongrel" depicted on the stamp is Babe, whose mother was a Labrador retriever. She belonged to Norman Todhunter, who designed the stamp (1).

Several other countries have issued stamps to honor their humane societies. The first was Cuba; in 1957, it issued a set of two— one regular and the other an air mail— to honor Mrs. Jeanette Ryder, founder of the Humane Society of Cuba (2). A set of four stamps (one of which is shown here) was issued in 1962 for the Surinam Organization for Animal Protection (3), and the Vienna Humane Society was honored with an Austrian stamp in 1966 (4). There have been other stamps issued for animal protection, a recent addition to the gallery being an outstanding four-stamp set is-sued in 1971 by Australia for the centenary of the Royal Society for Prevention of Cruelty to Animals.

France has issued a couple of stamps in honor of the profession. The 1951 issue in honor of veterinary medicine depicts the Veterinary College at Lyons (the first veterinary school, established in 1762), and professors E. Nocard, H. Bouley, and J. B. A. Chaveau (5). Nocard, in 1898, discovered the virus of psittacosis, which is now known eponymically as Nocardosis. In 1888, he had described bovine farcy, which also bears his eponym. Bouley, today considered one of the best authorities in the diagnoses and treatment of animal diseases, was Chief of Service at Alfort at the age of 23, and later became Inspector General of all French Animal Husbandry Schools. He was elected to the French Academy of Medicine and served as its president. Chaveau, who studied under Bouley, is best known for his investigation of heat and energy relations in muscular work, and for his "Retention Theory."

France's other stamp for the profession was issued in 1967 for the two hundredth an-niversary of the Alfort Veterinary School. It depicts Gaston Ramon and, if you look closely

10   2   4

8   1   5

3   9   7   6

11   12   13

at the stamp, you will see a statue which is that of Claude Bourgelat (6). Ramon, renowned for his work on the immunizations against tetanus and diphtheria, was a member of the French Academy of Sciences and Director of the Pasteur Institute. His acceptance of the E. Behring Prize in 1912 from the University of Marburg brought him a post-World War II charge of collaboration with the Germans, but he was later exonerated of this charge. Bourgelat (1712-1779) laid the foundation for veterinary medicine which was then an empiric discipline. He was a prolific writer. His *Medicine des Animaux*, published in 1760, led to the establishment of the Veterinary College at Lyons. The one hundred and twenty-fifth anniversary of Turkish veterinary medicine was commemorated by a set of two stamps issued in 1967.

Other veterinarians honored with stamps include Ignac Josef Pesina, a pioneer in veterinary medicine who was honored with a stamp issued by Czechoslovakia, and Dr. Fernec Hutyra, honored by Hungary as the founder of Hungarian veterinary medicine (7). The veterinarian Dauda Kairaba Jawara is shown on the stamps of Gambia. Graduated as D.V.M. in Scotland, in 1958 he was appointed Principal Veterinary Officer of Gambia, the highest post a native could hold. Then, entering politics, he rose to become president of the country.

Veterinary colleges have been honored on stamps. A 1958 stamp of Denmark commemorates the centenary of the Veterinary and Agricultural School, Copenhagen; the fiftieth anniversary of the Veterinary Medical Faculty at Zagreb was honored with a stamp of Jugoslavia; and Austria so commemorated the two hundredth anniversary of the Veterinary Medical School in Vienna. Upper Volta issued a stamp in 1970 for its National School of Veterinary Diseases (8), and Mali has issued stamps to publicize the Sotuba Zootechnical Institute (9).

Professional gatherings honored with stamps add several postal miniatures to the gallery. There is the largest "veterinary stamp," issued in 1969 for the first conference of the Arab Veterinary Union at Baghdad (10). Iran issued a stamp in 1967 for the Second Iranian Veterinary Congress and another one in 1971 for the Fourth Iranian Veterinary Congress at Teheran. The Eighth Arab Veterinary Congress in Cairo is commemorated with a stamp of Egypt (U.A.R.) issued in 1968.

A sizeable number of African countries have issued colorful stamps to publicize the campaign to control Rinderpest. Several of these interesting designs are shown on page 146 (11, 12, 13).

The gallery of veterinary stamps is fairly large. There are stamps issued by various countries to publicize better cattle breeding, and there are stamps depicting and publicizing the meat packing industry, canning, tanning, and various subjects which relate to different facets of animal life with which the veterinarian is closely allied. The gallery may be enlarged by inclusion of stamps depicting famous personalities connected with animal studies— Pavlov, Koch, Pasteur, and others.

Diligent study of stamps can turn up many unusual ones related to the veterinary profession. For example, one veterinarian, the world famous Jean Marie Camille-Guérin, is honored indirectly. His initial, the "G," is shown on the BCG stamp issued by France in honor of his co-worker, Albert Calmette. Another related stamp can be that of Iraq, depicting Hammurabi. The Code set fees for "doctor(s) of oxen or asses." How were the fees? So-So. An ox or ass cured commanded a sixth of a shekel of silver, but a sheep healed was paid for in kind: A dinner of meat was set as the fee.

49. Weight Lifting

For many years, weight lifting was one of the least represented sports on stamps. In 1959, there were only six of them: two Russian and one each Chinese, Hungarian, Japanese, and Persian. Ten years later, there were 58 stamps issued by 34 nations and each year sees more of them appear.

The world's first weight lifting stamp was issued by Russia in 1949 and today Russia still leads in this category with Hungary running a close second. While most of these stamps in the past were issued for the Olympics, the trend is now to issue them to commemorate national and international weight lifting competitions. They are also being included in stamp sets issued to publicize physical fitness, which was the motif of the world's first weight lifting stamp.

The first stamp issued to publicize an all weight lifting event— a "pure" weight lifting stamp— was the Persian (Iran) stamp of 1957 issued for their national championships. In 1965, Persia issued another stamp, this one to commemorate the World Weight Lifting Championships at Teheran. Hungary has issued several weight lifting stamps for the various Olympiads and also, in 1962, it issued a single for the European Weight Lifting Championships. The 1966 International and European Weight Lifting Championships in Berlin were honored on two East German stamps.

Many Asian nations have issued weight lifting stamps. Red China has issued several of them. Indonesia issued a weight lifting stamp as part of the set for the Fourth Asian Games at Djakarta in 1962. Japan issued a couple of weight lifting stamps, the first one back in 1958. South Korea issued one for the 1960 Olympics.

Latin American countries are now joining in with weight lifting issues also. Mexico, Costa Rica, and Haiti have issued them, and in 1971 Peru joined with a stamp for the XXVth World Weight Lifting Championships at Lima.

Other countries which have issued weight lifting stamps include British Guiana, Jamaica, Albania, Bulgaria, Congo Republic, Portuguese Angola, Lebanon, Morocco, Qatar, Sharjah, and many others.

The growing importance of weight lifting all over the world was clearly shown by postage stamps issued for the 1972 Olympiad in Munich. No less than ten nations issued Olympic stamps depicting weight lifting. From Russia, where weight lifting is a national sport, came the world's first souvenir sheet to depict weight lifting.

A souvenir sheet of Trinidad and Tobago issued for the 1972 Olympics contains two weight lifting stamps commemorating medals won in 1948 and in 1952. This is also the first time that weight lifting stamps have been included in a souvenir sheet containing other sports stamps.

Another memorable weight lifting tribute included in the 1972 Olympic issues is the stamp of Bulgaria. It was first issued as an "ordinary" weight lifting stamp, then to celebrate Bulgaria's gold medalist it was re-issued in November 1972 with a gold overprint reading "The First in the World." A stamp like this has appeared previously, honoring the 1968 Japanese gold medal weight lifter Yoshinobu Miyake, but it was issued by the Trucial States sheikdom of Fujeira, which does not participate in the Games and whose stamps were mainly produced for sale to collectors and not for actual postal use. The Bulgarian stamp, however, could be the beginning of a new trend to depict individual medalists.

Other nations which issued weight lifting stamps for the 1972 Olympics include Burundi, Egypt—which showed the official sign used to depict weight lifting— Korea, Mongolia, Poland, Portuguese Guinea, and Spain.

Various interesting weight lifting stamps exist. One is a Russian stamp issued for the 1968 Olympics in Mexico. It is unusual in that it shows three weight lifting positions. Only one other stamp like this is known, though there are some showing two positions or two weight lifters. (The first weight lifting stamps all depicted the completed jerk; it was only much later that other movements were added.)

Another unusual item (shown on the photo page) is the stamp issued by Samoa for the Third Pacific Games, at Port Moresby, Papua and New Guinea, August 13-23, 1969. Obviously, either the designer of the stamp never saw a weight lifter or else his model was truly powerful in the elbows!

Another interesting item comes from Japan. It is a special post card issued by the Japan Stamp Bureau for the Thirteenth National Athletic Meeting, Toyama Prefecture. It is franked with the stamp issue for the occasion and cancelled with a special commemorative cancellation. On the right, a figure of the weight lifter and his weight record are shown in colors.

50. Yachting and Boating

For the water sports enthusiast, the enormous gallery of boating stamps can be an interesting and challenging topic. There is something for everybody in this gallery, since sailing has been shown on stamps of almost all nations that can claim a large body of water. Sailboats of every kind have appeared on stamps in sufficient variety to form a collection of almost all the different types of sailboats extant. Many of the island nations, and those bordering the oceans, have issued stamps showing their native crafts.

Yachting, power and sail, has been depicted by the stamps of over 100 nations. One can put together an interesting collection of these miniatures, some which have been issued for specific events, while others were issued merely to stress the pleasures of yachting. Depictions of yacht races alone can form an entire collection, and just the yachts of the rich and famous could form a small and interesting one. Of course, there is more to collecting stamps than just arranging them on album pages. You learn your subject as you go along, and you'll find that many have studied it before, leaving you voluminous literature on which to base your collection. Many interesting things can be learned in the course of

building your collection. For example, the world's first yachting stamp issued for a specific yachting event is a stamp of The Netherlands issued for the 1928 Olympics. But the yacht shown on this stamp is a cutter, a type of boat not represented in the Olympics! Or, take the 1956 Bermuda stamp depicting the 6-meter racing yacht "Lucie." The "Lucie" was not, as popularly supposed, a Bermuda yacht but belonged to Mr. S. Briggs Cunningham of Connecticut. It was intended that the Bermuda yacht "Viking," owned by Mr. Kenneth Trimingham, be depicted, but somehow a mistake was made.

Memorable yacht journeys have been honored with special stamps. In 1967, Great Britain commemorated Sir Francis Chichester's one-man voyage around the world with a stamp depicting his yacht, the "Gipsy Moth IV." It is the only yachting stamp ever issued by Great Britain, though she has issued many of them for use in her various colonies and possessions. A three-year voyage around the world by the ocean-going yacht "Alferez Campora" is another instance of a special issue; in this case, two stamps were issued by Uruguay in 1963.

Is motor boating your fancy? If so, you can

start your collection with a Russian stamp issued in 1948 as a part of sports on stamps series. Russia has issued many motor boating stamps, since it is a very popular sport there. Of course, you can include in your collection motor boats used for other than sports purposes. You'll find many motor boat stamps issued for various naval activities long before the sports issue. The latest unusual motor boat stamp is a 1970 issue of East Germany depicting two policemen in a speed boat. It was issued to honor the twenty-fifth anniversary of the founding of their People's Police — the dreaded Vopos. Other motor boats appear on stamps issued to promote tourism or to show fishing or water skiing.

Water skiing is a newcomer to stamp designs and not many exist, but there are all indications that it has been well received and many more such stamps can be expected in the future. Some of these stamps show motor boats towing the skiiers; on others, the skier is there but the boat is absent. Since you can't water ski without a motor boat, these stamps might reasonably be included in a collection of motor boating. One such stamp exists showing a kite skier, high in the air.

Fishing is another big gallery. You can just about show anything you want to, though you yourself have to make the distinction between commercial and sport fishing, as many of these stamps just depict fishing and leave unsaid whether it's business or pleasure.

Rowing, introduced into the Olympics in 1900, is one of the fastest growing sports stamp designs. At least 40 countries have issued stamps depicting rowing. Another very popular design is canoeing, which achieved Olympic status in 1924. Some 55 countries have shown it on nearly 500 stamps. Just one country, Papua (formerly British New Guinea), has issued 142 stamps showing their native canoe, the lakatoi. There are even stamps that depict surf boating.

American entries in the boating gallery are not too numerous. There's "Breezing Up," by Winslow Homer, on the 1962 commemorative issued in his honor (the original hangs in the National Gallery of Art in Washington); there's "The Boating Party," on the 1966 Mary Cassatt commemorative (original also in the National Gallery), and the 1967 stamp issued in honor of Thomas Eakins, which reproduced another painting from the National Gallery, "The Biglin Brothers Racing" (it shows sculling on Schuylkill River, Philadelphia). There are also sailboats, or yachts, on some of the American stamps issued for use in the Canal Zone. In addition, there are boats, small and large, on various other American stamps and some of those might just fit your favorite theme.

51. How to Form a Topical Stamp Collection

Selecting a topic is the most important decision you will make in forming a collection. Obviously your topic must be one that interests you, perhaps one related to your work or profession, some other hobby, or a field that has continually fascinated you.

For example, doctors often collect medical stamps. An athlete may run the gamut of Sports on Stamps. An active Lion or Rotarian may select stamps honoring his organization. A gardener, bird watcher, railroad buff or boat fan, each will find topics related to his interest. Other topics are suggested by the stamp illustrations in this book. Actually, the possibilities are unlimited.

A solution is to select a topic, within a larger topic, for which you have acquired a special liking. For instance, your larger topic may be animals, but you are particularly attracted to the cat family. You can concentrate on lions, tigers, alley cats, and kittens. If you have already accumulated other animal stamps, retain them. After you have exhausted the cats you may want to try another animal clan, or you may decide to use your excess animal stamps as trading bait.

Once you select your topic, the rest is easy. If there is a stamp dealer in your city (see your phone directory) visit him and purchase a packet of stamps covering the topic you decided to collect. You will find that all the popular topics are available in the form of packets. If the dealer is out of your topic, he may be able to order a packet for you. If there is no stamp dealer where you live you can get it by mail from a specialist mail-order dealer. All larger newsstands carry stamp collector's magazines and these publications list hundreds of mail-order dealers and their specialties.

Buy the largest packet you can afford to buy—they come in all sizes, from 25 different stamps to 500 different stamps, and even larger, if the subject is very big. While in the stamp store, pick up a cheap stamp album, with 8-1/2x11-inch blank pages (or buy 3-hole-punched white pages and a binder in any store that carries stationery). A small expenditure of time and money will get you started.

Suppose you selected as your topic Flowers on Stamps. Take your "paper flowers" home. Look at them, enjoy them, sort them as you

154

wish by color or country, by species or season of bloom, by habitat or personal choice. Arrange them on album pages, 10 to 15 to a page, add a few words of description, and you've become a collector of Flowers on Stamps!

Go as far as you wish: Add stamps picturing birds and butterflies to your garden, or add a pool of tropical fish. There's no limit to your garden with stamps; you're not bound by type of soil or climate, only by your imagination.

This, of course, is only a very basic collection—a beginner's way of doing it, and after a few months of experiment you may decide to enlarge the collection or to dig deeper into the subject. Once you decide to really "go after" it, you will have to obtain some basic checklists and handbooks so that you can take advantage of the work done by others in locating appropriate stamps, because once you pass out of the beginner-stage you will find the stamps you need are no longer available in packets. Then, you might also want to look into the possibility of buying some catalogs and some specialized stamp albums and supplies which will improve the looks of the collection. Last, but not least by any means, you'll probably want to join a stamp club. Most collectors do.

In the next chapter you will find information on where to obtain stamps, catalogs, and supplies. In Chapter 53, you will find complete information on all checklists and handbooks and that all-important information on how to join your fellow topical collectors in a stamp club.

52. Where to Get Stamps, Stamp Catalogs, Albums, and Supplies

Readers living in cities in which stamp dealers have stores are not necessarily assured of being able to buy from them all the stamps which they will need for their selected topics. This is true even of very large cities with a great many stamp stores.

The reason for this is that most of the stamp dealers who specialize in topicals are mail order dealers— often part-timers who used to be collectors of the very same topics in which they now specialize as dealers. These specialist dealers have a lot of material that stamp stores don't handle, for the simple reason that to maintain such a specialized stock requires a countrywide clientele. But specialists in a hundred topics are as near to you as your nearest mailbox; all you have to do is find their addresses.

It's easy to locate a mail order specialist if you know where to look for him. The very best place to look is between the covers of *Topical Time* magazine, the official publication of the American Topical Association. This 100-page magazine carries 140 advertisements of all kinds of topical specialists in each issue—from a man who sells only ships on stamps, through a fellow who handles nothing but chess, and on to a dealer who carries 40 different topics in various-sized packets.

The next best bet in locating the topical dealers are two stamp magazines widely sold by the larger newsstands and available at many public libraries: *Linn's Stamp News* and *Stamps*. The first is a large, thick tabloid; the other is a slim news magazine-size weekly. Both publications carry advertisements by topical specialists, particularly in their classified pages. Of the two, *Linn's* is the better to look to for topicalists. If your town does not have a news dealer who carries either of these weeklies, and if it's not at your library, write to the publishers for a sample copy (enclose postage):

Linn's Weekly Stamp News
P.O. Box 29
Sydney, Ohio 45365

Stamps
153 Waverly Place
New York, New York 10014

Readers in Great Britain and South Africa can obtain *Stamp Collecting* (42 Maiden Lane, London WC2E 7LL), and readers in Australia and New Zealand are directed to *Australian Stamp News* (Sterling Street, Dubbo, N.S.W.). Canadian readers can obtain United States publications on their newsstands or by mail.

Catalogs, albums, and supplies are obtained with greater ease than stamps. Stamp stores carry most popular items (or can, and will, obtain them for their customers), and anything missing is easily obtainable by mail from ads in the above-mentioned publications.

Because topical collecting has no set of strict rules, the choice of album is wide open and most collectors use some kind or another of a blank page. However, some of the more popular topics—chess, medicine, flowers, space, to mention just a few—can also be housed in special albums on special pages prepared by specialists. Some of these topical albums are available only from one or two specialists (for example, pages for Masonry or for chess) and these specialized supplies are seldom offered in general stamp publications. You'll have to look for them in *Topical Time.*

Stamp catalogs do not list stamps according to topics, but by country, date of issue, and type of issue. However, stamp catalogs are the basic tools for topical collectors because their stamp numbers are used in advertisements, price lists, articles, checklists, and topical handbooks. Catalogs are available in most public libraries and in many regular book stores as well as through all stamp dealers.

The basic catalog used in the United States and Canada is the "Scott" catalog, formally known as the *Standard Postage Stamp Catalogue,* published in three volumes each year by the Scott Publishing Company, New York, N.Y. Most catalog numbers used in magazine advertising and price lists and in handbooks issued in the United States are Scott numbers. Another American catalog gaining in popularity is known as the "Minkus" catalog, a two-volume annual publication by Minkus Publications, Inc., New York, N.Y., formally titled the *Minkus New World-Wide Postage Stamp Catalog.* Though not as useful for buying stamps as Scott, Minkus is a good catalog for the topicalist, as it has many more illustrations.

In other English-speaking countries, the basic catalog is the "Gibbons," by Stanley Gibbons, Ltd. of London. Gibbons is available in various formats. The best for the topicalist is the thick, one-volume *Stamps of the World,* which used to be called the "Simplified." It's an excellent catalog, well worth having in one's topical library. Superb catalogs are available in all languages, particularly in German and in French, and in all countries.

Though there exist some catalogs of certain topics, none exists in the English language and none has attained great popularity, with the possible exception of an Italian catalog covering the subject of "Europa." However, there exist more than a hundred books and handbooks in English which list the stamps of the various topics, and these indispensable topicalists' helpers are listed in the next chapter.

53. Where to Get Handbooks, Checklists, and Other Topical Information

The *easiest* way to enter topical stamp collecting is to join the American Topical Association. The non-profit, Milwaukee-based ATA is the largest world-wide society of topical stamp collectors, with nearly 11,000 members in 90 different countries. The ATA issues *Topical Time*, the world's foremost publication on topicals, which is sent to all members bi-monthly. Printed on heavy gloss enamel coated paper, and lavishly illustrated, it has nearly 100 pages per issue of articles, topical checklists, news and views on a wide variety of topical subjects, and notes of interest to members. Articles give the story behind the stamp and they're written in a down-to-earth manner to appeal to all, not to a mere handful of specialists. Simple, step-by-step articles by recognized experts and by exhibition winners tell you how to arrange, write up, and mount your topical collection. A computerized topical new issue section lists issues in alphabetical topical order under 117 subject headings. Stamp dealers specializing in topicals advertise heavily in *Topical Time,* making it easy to locate exactly what one needs for the collection.

The ATA membership directory has nearly 200 pages. Officers, committees, regular members are all listed, along with their collecting specialties and their addresses. An important feature for the newcomer wishing to find kindred spirits for exchanging information and trading stamps is the listing of members under the 700 different topics they collect as well as some 200 countries and other specialties which members collect. A 600-member Information Board is listed to answer your questions on more than 280 different topical subjects.

Numerous study and research units, devoted to special topics such as Americana, art, aviation, biology, Christmas, Churchill, communications, education, engineering, Europa, geology, journalism, Judaica, law and lawyers, Lions International, maps, Masonry, medical subjects, music, performing arts, railroads, Red Cross, Roosevelt, Rotary, Scouts, ships, space, sports, stamps on stamps and centenaries, theatre, United Nations, etc., offer opportunities for association with people with the same interests as the new member. Most of the units publish bulletins, and all conduct research and prepare much of the material appearing in *Topical Time.*

Chapters of the American Topical Association exist in many cities, on four continents, and new ones are constantly being formed. Chapters usually have monthly meetings and programs for their members; some stage exhibits and issue bulletins. The ATA also holds shows where members may exhibit their collections for a trophy, and participates with gold, silver, and bronze medals and award certifications for topical collections at many national, regional, and local stamp shows.

A sales service offers an easy and inexpensive way to dispose of topical duplicates for cash, and to add hard-to-get items to the collection. It is the only all-topical sales service in the world, with one topic mounted to a book.

Membership in the ATA is open to all interested in topical collecting. ATA's nominal dues and initiation fee represent a big value for your money, particularly because members not only receive *Topical Time* but can also buy ATA-issued handbooks at special prices. The ATA has issued over 100 handbooks on various topics and some of those which relate to some of the chapters in this book are listed below. For a complete list of handbooks with member-prices and information on joining the ATA, write to:

American Topical Association
330 8Y North 50 Street
Milwaukee, Wisconsin 53216

Some of the 100 handbooks available from the ATA:

For Chapter 3: Handbook #57, *World Jet Aircraft on Stamps*

For Chapter 4: Handbook #58, *Americana on Foreign Stamps*

For Chapter 11: Handbook #82, *Birds of the World on Stamps*

For Chapter 18: Handbook #61, *Flowers on Stamps*

For Chapter 23: Handbook #52, *Horses on Stamps*

For Chapter 29: Handbook #59, *Lions International on Stamps*

For Chapter 30: Handbook #43, *Masonic Stamps of the World*

For Chapter 31: Handbook #39, *Medical History in Philately*

For Chapter 34: Handbook #37, *Music Philately Encyclopedia*

For Chapter 42: Handbook #80, *Watercraft Philately*

For Chapter 43: Handbook #54, *Space Stamps*

For Chapter 44: Handbook #83, *Sports and Recreation Checklist*

Collectors of *Judaica* can obtain a good checklist in form of a copy of the *International Judaica Philatelic Handbook,* from the S.A.R. Academy, 655 West 254 Street, Riverdale, New York 10471.

Besides the American Topical Association there exist several small, specialized topical collectors' societies which issue handbooks and publications covering their special interests. In Chapter 41, we mentioned the Scouts on Stamps Society International. For information on this organization write to Edward S. Hoffmeister, 422 So. 2 St., Colwyn, Darby, PA 19023, enclosing a stamped, self-addressed envelope.

About 650 collectors of religion on stamps are banded together in a Collectors of Religion on Stamps Society, popularly known as COROS. This organization publishes several handbooks and it issues a bi-monthly journal, *The Coros Chronicle.* Details on COROS may be had from Waller A. Sager, 6232 Annan Way, Los Angeles, CA 90042.

Some collectors of stamps related to sports and recreation belong to the Sports Philatelists International, which issues the *Journal of Sports Philately,* a bi-monthly covering all phases of this topic. Information can be obtained from Helen Long, 6073 Woodland, Apt. 26, Ventura, CA 93003.

Fine Arts Philatelists is an organization of collectors interested in any aspect of this large specialty. They publish a number of handbooks on various specialized topics, such as, for example, archaeology, paintings, and sculptures, and issue the *FAP Journal,* a bi-monthly devoted to the various fine arts topics. Information can be had from John S. Papa, 1950 N.E. 59 Place, Fort Lauderdale, FL 33308.

ABOUT THE AUTHOR

M. W. Martin is one of the world's leading writers on philatelic subjects, having written more than 400 articles and columns for popular magazines, trade and professional magazines, and house organs in the United States, Canada, England, Australia, South Africa and New Zealand. He also writes popular presentations of medical and technological developments, and has published two books in this area, *Let's Talk About the New World of Medicine,* and *Miracles in Medicine.* A stamp collector since boyhood, Mr. Martin has managed to combine his vocation to produce stories illustrating the pleasures of his hobby. He is a member of many stamp societies and a Life Member of the American Topical Association.